Pastor Gail -

God Bless you
and your Family -

Anne Sandel
1 COR 15:58

BROKENNESS

BROKENNESS

HOW GOD REDEEMS PAIN AND SUFFERING

LON SOLOMON

RED DOOR
PRESS

Potomac, MD

Brokenness:
How God Redeems Pain and Suffering
By Lon Solomon
© 2006
First Edition / 5th Printing

Published by Red Door Press, Inc.
Silver Spring, MD
(301) 588-7599
RedDoorPress@comcast.net

ISBN-13: 978-0-9763770-0-9
ISBN-10: 0-9763770-0-4
LCCN 2004099535

Cover design and illustration by Dan Rebeiz

Interior design by Pneuma Books, LLC
visit www.pneumabooks.com for more information

11 10 09   9 8 7

To my special gift from God, my daughter, Jill

Thanks to you I have learned lessons
I would have never learned any other way.
Your presence in my life has made me
a better man, a better husband,
a better father, and a better pastor.

Thank you, Jill, for living the life
God has called you to live
with such grace and enthusiasm.
I deeply respect your courage and your will
to fight on even through the most challenging
of circumstances.

Jill, I dedicate all the proceeds from this book
to supporting you and meeting your needs.

There is a great want about

all Christians who have not suffered.

Some flowers must be broken or bruised

before they emit any fragrance.

All the wounds of Christ

send out sweetness — all the sorrows

of Christians do the same.

~

Robert Murray McCheyne
in *Banner of Truth Trust*

PREFACE

In the fall of 2004, I was in a Cairo bazaar drinking bitter coffee with friends when a young Egyptian girl suddenly appeared before me. Cupped in her hands was a laminated card that she delicately pressed into my palm. On it were two sentences written in English. I looked at them and then at her, then back at the words: "I am deaf and dumb, but I am going to school to try and become self-sufficient in life. Could you please help me?"

It would have been easy to ignore her. But instinctively, I reached into my pocket and pulled out fifty Egyptian pounds, about eight American dollars, and placed it in her soiled fingers. Before I could withdraw my hand, she embraced it, kissing the top, then rubbing her face on it, alternating between each gesture for what seemed like several minutes.

I was feeling flush in the face and uncomfortable at this act of kindness and gratitude from the young girl kneeling before me. The more I tried to pull my hand away, the more she caressed it. In her own way, she was thanking me for caring enough to give her something that could help, not just a few pennies. The only regret I have was not giving her more.

If this had happened in 1992, I would have done what many people were doing to her — handed the card right back. But you see, for the last twelve years I have lived with a little girl who is now about the same age as the child in the bazaar. My daughter's name is Jill. And it was her face and her struggles that popped into my mind when the Egyptian girl handed me that card.

This book is based on an intensely personal relationship with Jill. Its tenets were learned in the fires of deep suffering. God taught me the truths of this book at the bottom of the worst emotional black hole that I've experienced in fifty-six years of living. I can certify that the precepts in this book are, as David says in Psalm 19:9, sure and altogether trustworthy, because I have lived them.

My wife Brenda and I had always wanted a daughter. As Brenda was turning forty, we had three healthy, wonderful boys — but no little girl. So we resigned ourselves that a daughter was out of the question. Then one day, Brenda came to me with the news: she was pregnant. It was unexpected and unplanned, and when we learned the baby was a girl, we were ecstatic.

For the first three months of her life, Jill was a normal, healthy baby. Then we noticed something wrong with her arms. They were twitching, a malady we soon learned had a name: focal seizures. We were scared and worried, fearful of what might happen next to Jill. We prayed for the best, but the worst happened. Her localized seizures evolved into full-body, grand mal convulsions. By the time Jill was a year old, she was having multiple major seizures daily.

We saw doctor after doctor and tried every type of medicine. Nothing worked. The experts suggested trying the Ketogenie diet, a radical, high-fat diet pioneered by Johns Hopkins Hospital. Still, the seizures kept on coming. Sometimes Jill would have as many as twelve grand mal seizures in a day.

The rescue squad arrived so many times at our house we knew each paramedic by name. They'd race in, insert a valium drip intravenously into Jill's arm, then rush her to the emergency room. At the hospital, the doctors would carry her into a room and pull the drapes closed, cutting us off from any view of our child. We would be told to stay outside, leaving us unknowing what was going on behind the drapes. We hoped and prayed Jill was fighting for her life. And we cried.

These episodes were so serious that Jill had to stay for several days in the pediatric intensive care unit.

Brenda and I would be with her, sleeping in chairs in the care unit's waiting room. On Jill's first Thanksgiving Day she had nineteen grand mal seizures. We spent the entire weekend in the hospital with her.

In 2000, she almost died from a rash of uncontrollable seizures. With heavy hearts, Brenda and I began to plan her funeral service. Despite the odds, Jill survived but lost the ability to walk, stand up on her own or even sit in a chair without falling over.

To date, Jill has had nearly six thousand seizures that have profoundly damaged her brain and left her severely mentally retarded. Yet, to our dismay, none of the doctors who had been treating Jill were able to tell us exactly what was wrong with her. One doctor summed it up this way: "Well, she's got a nasty seizure disorder."

Finally, in God's amazing mercy, we met Dr. Richard Kelley at the Kennedy-Kreiger Genetics Institute at Johns Hopkins Medical Center. Dr. Kelley evaluated Jill and said right off, "I believe I know what's wrong with Jill. She has mitochondrial disease." He explained that it's a genetic problem that keeps the body from producing enough energy to meet its needs, and one of the major symptoms is massive numbers of seizures. "It's like the brain is running on low-test fuel," Dr. Kelley told us, "so it pings and knocks and has seizures."

Jill's disorder, he said, could not be cured. It could be treated though, by a cocktail of energy-enhancing vitamins and anti-oxidants. Jill began this regimen in 2000 and her improvement has been nothing short of miraculous. She has gone from nearly twelve seizures a day to one every two to four weeks. She has regained all of her mobility and has even begun to learn some new skills.

Nonetheless, the damage from thousands of seizures has left Jill severely impaired. She has lost the ability to speak, which she once could do, and is now completely nonverbal. She is not potty trained, nor can she dress herself. She recognizes her family, but she cannot understand even simple commands or grasp even the most elementary concepts. If she kicks the covers off during the night, she will lie in the fetal position and shiver, unaware of her need to simply pull the blankets over her. If she went outside in cold weather and became chilled, she could not fathom the idea that a coat would warm her.

Jill has no conception of danger, and for her protection, someone must watch her every minute of every day for the rest of her life. Apart from a miracle from the Lord, Brenda and I will be caring for Jill until we or she passes away.

The impact of Jill's sickness has been devastating for us. We had to watch our little girl suffer so badly while we were powerless to help her. Then there was the physical and emotional exhaustion we experienced. Jill didn't sleep through the night for eight years, from 1992 through 2000. She would have seizures through the night, which required hourly care or trips to the emergency room. We were walking zombies for those years — exhausted, spent, and burned out.

On top of this, we had three boys to care for. Jamie was fourteen when Jill was born; Justin was eleven and Jon was six. Jill consumed so much of our time and energy that we had little left to give the boys. We tried our best to get to their ballgames, help with their homework, play games with them, take them on vacations, be involved with their spiritual lives, and support them through their teenage years. But we always felt we were failing them. The guilt from this was terrible. We felt like we were in a lose-lose situation and there was absolutely no light at the end of the tunnel.

Then there was the grief — the grief of watching our dreams and plans for our little girl vanish. There would be no shopping trips to the mall, where Brenda and Jill could laugh and buy clothes. There would be no piano lessons, dance lessons, first dates, prom nights, or teaching Jill to drive. I was never going to walk my daughter down the aisle or watch her become a mother.

All of our dreams for our own life would never be fulfilled either. There would be no empty nest days when we could travel together and enjoy one another's company unencumbered by the demands of children. There would be no impulsive dinners out or dashes to the movie theater to catch a last-minute showing. The plans we had cherished for what life would be like in our fifties and beyond were now dead, forever. The loss of our future was an utterly shattering blow to us. The strains on our marriage were at times unbearable.

So I began to ask some hard questions: Where is God in all of this? Why would he allow this to happen to me when I am trying so hard to serve him faithfully? Is God really engaged in this suffering, or am I just at the mercy of these circumstances? I know Romans 8:28 says that God works for the good of those who love him, but what good can possibly come out of the pain Brenda and I are suffering through? Am I a bad Christ follower with some serious sins in my life that God is punishing me for, even though I can't figure out what they might be? Am I a follower of Christ at all? Have I been deceiving myself all along? Is my faith somehow insufficient?

This book is the result of twelve years of such questions, studying God's Word for answers, and watching God redeem our pain and turn it into good, just as he promised. I have seen God redeem the suffering that our family has experienced in ways that I could never have imagined twelve years ago.

Jill's disability has been a defining moment for me as a father and a husband. Today, Brenda and I have a much stronger marriage. And Jill has made me a better pastor, providing me the foresight to want to help others with disabilities. Brenda and I will be serving Jill for the rest of our lives. Instead of considering it a burden, we consider it a privilege.

I have learned about brokenness and have understood its power firsthand. And I now realize that had I better known the principles in this book, I would have gone through the last twelve years with far more hope, far more assurance, and far less anguish of the soul.

If you're a follower of Christ, and you're going through a time of deep suffering and pain, the message in this book will help you, as it did me, understand why God breaks us before he can fully use us. I believe it will bring you hope and reassurance. I pray this book will give you a spiritual perspective on what is happening to you, one that is both biblical and time-tested.

As David said in Psalm 23, I hope this book will restore your soul.

Lon Solomon
November 4, 2004

CONTENTS

Foreword by Tim LaHaye xxiii

1. What's the Real Question 1
2. Every Exodus Needs a Moses. 19
3. Reducing Our Resistance 31
4. Embracing the Product,
   Resisting the Process 57
5. Opening a Hole in the Defensive Line 83
6. The Product Is Worth the Process 103

Epilogue 129
Acknowledgments 137
About the Author 141

FOREWORD

By Dr. Tim LaHaye

Many years ago, while on a skiing trip, I received the good news that our youngest daughter had just given birth to her fourth child. My wife Beverly and I were ecstatic to say the least. Two nights later, Lori called again, but this time her tone had changed dramatically and she was weeping uncontrollably. "Stephen has been diagnosed with Downs Syndrome." Needless to say, from that moment on, her life, along with the lives of her husband (who was a Christian school principal) and their three other children would be forever altered.

Through her tears, she asked the most common of all questions under the circumstances, "Daddy, why me?" I had already quietly asked God the same thing, "Lord, why her?" Both Lori and her husband had played the game of life just the way God teaches they should. They were active in their local church and had dedicated their children to the Lord. They were both Christian college graduates. They had met at a Christian summer camp where they were both counselors. Both taught at a Christian school. Most importantly, they loved the Lord with all their hearts. Why would he let this happen to them?

As a pastor for thirty-seven years, I have not only had to answer that question for myself, but for those in my congregation who experienced similar tragedies. The truth is, nearly all of us at one time or another have had to face devastating situations. I believe Lon Solomon, author of this amazing and inspiring book, is uniquely qualified to answer the difficult questions. He is the pastor of a highly influential church in Washington, D.C., and he too has experienced life's heartaches firsthand.

Lon Solomon believes, as I do, that the Bible has solutions to the problems of life. Recognized as an outstanding Bible teacher, he is also known for his practical application of the Word of God in everyday situations. In *Brokenness*, Lon Solomon gives biblical answers to tough questions like these: Does God himself actually send trouble and pain into the lives of his followers or is he simply a passive observer? Does God bring about difficulty as a punishment for sin? Does God *inflict* people with disease or does he simply *allow* it? Ultimately, is it God or Satan who is responsible for the suffering we face?

Obviously, what we believe about God greatly affects our relationship with him. Therefore, it is vital that we each have a biblically accurate view of the true nature of God. In my opinion, *Brokenness* provides important and life-changing insights into the ways of God. At the same time, it cuts through the misinformation that has been taught for so many years by the misguided and misinformed.

This book will prove to be a valuable resource indeed, for anyone who has experienced the pain and suffering of this world and asked, "Why me, God,"

A NOTE
From Lon Solomon

This book is for people who have made a decision to trust Jesus Christ as their personal Lord and Savior. For those of you who have not yet done so, I urge you to visit our website at McLean Bible Church (www.mcleanbible.org) and listen to the story of how I, a Jewish person, came to faith in Jesus as Messiah.

I challenge you to consider the claims of Christ on your life. I want to urge you to give your life to him like I did in 1971. It was the best decision I've ever made, and it transformed my life into something worth getting up for each morning. As Jesus said in John 10:10, he gives his followers not just life, but abundant life.

Once a person has embraced Jesus as their personal Savior, a deep, rich, and intimate relationship with the living God of the universe is possible. Brokenness is the pathway that we must walk in order to get such a relationship with God.

If you're not sure you understand this concept, or that you even agree with it, then I invite you to read on.

Commend me to a bruised brother, a broken reed —
for the Man of Sorrows is never far from him.
To me, there is something sacred and sweet
in all suffering, for it is so much akin
to the Man of Sorrows

~Robert Murray McCheyne
in *Banner of Truth Trust*~

CHAPTER ONE

WHAT'S THE REAL QUESTION?

I sat quietly in my office listening to a young couple explain their situation. They told me about their child who had recently been born with multiple disabilities. The doctors' prognostications were bleak. Their newborn child would be severely handicapped, mentally and physically, for life.

They held hands and struggled to speak, often deferring to each other when one of them became too choked up to keep talking. "Pastor Lon, why would God allow something like this to happen to us?" the young wife asked.

"We have both dedicated our lives to Christ," her husband said. "We have tried to find areas where we could serve God. We've contributed faithfully to the work of God. We're trying to live lives of obedience to

God every day. I don't understand why God would send something like this to us."

With tears in their eyes, they looked at me, hoping for an answer that would make some sense — an answer that would bring some order to their confusion and pain. This was not an unfamiliar scene for me. As a pastor for more than twenty-five years, people in my office have asked me this same question more times than I can remember.

WHAT'S THE REAL QUESTION?

Notice that this couple's question was not, "Why does God send pain and suffering to people in our world?" Most followers of Christ understand that one of God's eternal principles in the Bible is that "a man reaps what he sows" (Gal 6:7b). So, if they can see some wrong action on their part that precipitated their pain and suffering, most Christ-followers will accept that their wrong action is a sensible explanation for that pain. Put very simply: they are merely suffering the human consequences for their actions — consequences that the Bible warned them about. Most followers of Christ can also accept this principle as the explanation for a large amount of the pain and suffering that they see around them in other people's lives.

On an even deeper level spiritually, Christ-followers also understand that sometimes God disciplines his children as Hebrews 12:4-11 tells us. This means that, in any given situation, our suffering could be directly related to an area of our life where God is trying to get our attention — where he is trying to get us to repent and change our behavior. If Christ-followers can see — or if someone can point out to them — such an area in their lives, this too provides a sensible answer as to why they are experiencing pain and suffering.

But here's where the trouble began for the couple in my office. They were sincere followers of Christ who, when they examined their lives carefully, could find no infractions on either of these levels. To the best of their knowledge, they weren't engaging in any overt behaviors that should have produced the kind of devastating human consequence they were suffering. Nor, to the best of their knowledge, could they identify any areas of defiant disobedience or rebellion in their hearts that needed God's discipline.

Now, is it possible that they were deceiving themselves and that there really were some serious spiritual issues in their lives? Of course that's possible. But it's also possible they were telling the truth and that their assessment of themselves was correct.

If their assessment was correct — if they had no behavior patterns that produced such massive negative consequences or no defiant attitudes that deserved God's stiff discipline — then what's the answer to their question: "Why would God allow something like this to happen to us?"

Before we can answer this couple's question, we must first address an important theological issue. Namely, what is God's role when it comes to the pain, heartache and negative circumstances that come into a Christ-follower's life? Does God actually *send* trouble, pain, and tragedy into the lives of Christ-followers, or is he simply a passive observer who steps in to help us when these events come upon us?

Many preachers and theologians argue that God doesn't actively participate in sending negative things to his followers. They refer to the verse in the Bible that says, "Every good and perfect gift is from above, coming down from the Father of the heavenly lights" (James 1:17). Rather, they say, all the evil events that touch our lives come from the devil. The most God ever might do, they argue, is to *allow* the devil to do these evil things.

In this theological scenario, God offers to deliver us from these evil things. But since God himself doesn't send or orchestrate them, it is a waste of time for us to search for some spiritual reason *why* they have entered our life as Christ-followers. The simple answer is that Satan hates us as believers and is trying to destroy us.

According to this theological outlook, the answer to the question posed by the couple in my office is:

- Satan, not God, sent this situation your way to hurt your faith and damage your love for God.

- God actually had no direct part in sending this child with disabilities to you.
- This human tragedy has no overriding spiritual purpose.
- If God doesn't heal your child, then you just need to trust God to fulfill Romans 8:28 for you and turn all things into good for you and your child.

This theological outlook was popularized a few years ago in the book *Why Bad Things Happen To Good People* by Rabbi Harold S. Kushner. In this book, Rabbi Kushner says that God is essentially an uninvolved bystander when it comes to the negative and tragic circumstances that strike people's lives. God doesn't design these circumstances, nor does God approve of them. God's role is merely to help and succor us when these bad things come into our lives.

In my opinion, this entire theological understanding of how Almighty God relates to our tragedies, sorrows, and setbacks is biblically bogus.

WHAT THE BOOK OF JOB TEACHES US

In the first two chapters of the Book of Job, we find the most revealing account in the Bible of how God and Satan relate to the evil circumstances that enter the lives of God's followers.

The story is familiar to many, but let's review it anyway. Job is a godly man. He "is blameless and upright, a man who fears God and shuns evil" (Job 1:8b). As a result, the Lord had blessed Job's life in great ways.

One day, when Satan came before the Lord, the Lord boasted to Satan about Job's commitment to God. Satan challenged God's boast by saying, "Does Job fear God for nothing? Have you not put a hedge around him and his household and everything he has? You have blessed the work of his hands, so that his flocks and herds are spread throughout the land. But stretch out your hand and strike everything he has, and he will surely curse you to your face" (Job 1:9-11).

Here, Satan invited God to test Job's dedication to God. For the purpose of our discussion, the exact nature of Job's testing is not the issue. The issue for us is the level of involvement, or lack thereof, that God has in the tragedies and losses that Satan is allowed to inflict upon Job as a part of this testing.

Look at how God responds to Satan's challenge. "'Very well, then, everything Job has is in your hands, but on the man himself do not lay a finger.' Then Satan went out from the presence of the LORD" (Job 1:12).

Satan immediately orchestrated circumstances so that Job's farm animals, camels, and all of his servants but one were killed by marauding bands of Sabeans and Chaldeans. Furthermore, a house in which all of Job's children were eating collapsed because of bad weather, and all of Job's children died.

Yet the Bible says that Job's response was one of continuing trust in God. So Satan returned to God and asked for permission to inflict even greater suffering and pain on Job. He said, "Skin for skin! A man will give all he has for his own life. But stretch out your hand and strike his flesh and bones, and he will surely curse you to your face" (Job 2:4-5).

Once again, watch how God responds to Satan's request. "The Lord said to Satan, 'Very well, then, he is in your hands; but you must spare his life.' So Satan went our from the presence of the LORD and afflicted Job with painful sores from the soles of his feet to the top of his head" (Job 2:6-7).

The cogent points in Job chapters 1 and 2 for our consideration are these:

- It may have been Satan who actually inflicted upon Job the tragedies and losses Job suffered...
- It may have been Satan's desire and idea to abuse and hurt Job in these ways...
- It may have been Satan's motive, in doing all this, to destroy Job's trust in God...
- It may have been earthly instruments that Satan used to carry out his plans, like marauding bands and bad weather...
- *But* nothing was done to Job that had not first been inspected and authorized by Almighty God himself.

Please also notice that not only did God approve the negative circumstances that Satan was allowed to bring into Job's life, but God also set firm boundaries on these circumstances. This is critical, because it tells us that it was God, not Satan, who was ultimately in charge of what was happening in Job's life.

Notice, also, that when we look at Job's statements about his losses, it is clear that Job considered God to be the one who had personally sent these circumstances into his life.

In response to the loss of all his animals, servants, and children, Job said, "Naked I came from my mother's womb, and naked I will depart. The LORD gave and the LORD has taken away; may the name of the LORD be praised" (Job 1:21).

In response to the loss of his personal health, Job said, "Shall we accept good from God and not trouble?" (Job 2:10). He also said, "Though he slay me, yet will I hope in him"(Job 13:15).

It is clear from these statements that Job sees God as the source of his suffering. He sees these great losses come from the sovereign hand of God. In fact, Job hardly even acknowledges the instruments — namely, the marauding bands, the bad weather, or the hand of Satan — that God used to afflict him.

Later, in reflecting on the entire series of negative events that had occurred in his life, Job reaffirms this God-centered worldview of his affliction when he says:

Surely, O God, you have worn me out; you have devastated my entire household. God assails me and tears me in his anger. God has turned me over to evil men. All was well with me, but he shattered me; he seized me by the neck and crushed me. He has made me his target. Again and again he bursts upon me; he rushes at me like a warrior (*Job 16:7-14, excerpted*).

There can be no doubt that Job considered God himself to be the ultimate source of all the evil and tragedy that had come upon him. Job did not consider God to be an uninvolved bystander. Furthermore, Job did not perceive that God's only participation in these negative circumstances was that God *allowed* them. As far as Job was concerned, God personally did these things to him for reasons that Job struggled to understand.

THE WORLDVIEW OF THE REST OF THE BIBLE

One might argue that Job's worldview was simply wrong. So let's look at the rest of the Bible and see if it supports Job's worldview on this topic. In his Psalms, David is constantly calling out to God to help and succor him in trouble. David often talks about those troubles and where they come from. Listen to his worldview:

But now, you have rejected and humbled us;
you no longer go out with our armies.

You made us retreat before the enemy...
You gave us up to be devoured like sheep...
All this happened to us, though we had not for-
    gotten you or been false to your covenant.
Our hearts had not turned back;
our feet had not strayed from your path.
But you crushed us...and covered us over with
    deep darkness.
(*Ps 44:9-19, excerpted*)

Here we have a clear case of trouble striking David and the people of Israel, but not as a result of sin. David declares that the losses they had suffered on the battlefield could not be traced to either consequences of sin or godly discipline. Therefore, they were inexplicable in David's mind. But notice that as inexplicable as these negative circumstances might be David clearly attributes them directly and personally to God.

In Amos's prophecy, God says: "When disaster comes to a city, has not the Lord caused it?" (Amos 3:6). Regardless of the reason disaster strikes a city, or the exact instrument that carries out that disaster, God declares that it is he who ultimately caused it.

In Isaiah's great prophecy, chapters 40 through 46, God declares his awesome sovereignty over all the universe and every event in it. As part of his wonderful soliloquy in these chapters, God says:

I am the Lord, who has made all things,
who alone stretched out the heavens,
who spread out the earth by myself...
I am the Lord, and there is no other;
apart from me there is no God.
I form the light and create darkness,
I bring prosperity and create disaster;
I, the Lord, do all these things
(*Isa. 44:24 and 45:5a, 7*)

In the New Testament, we find this same worldview regarding God's direct role in tragedy, suffering, and troubles in the lives of Christ-followers. The Apostle Paul speaks about this in his second letter to the church of Corinth. Paul is speaking about the incredible revelations that God gave him and how God wanted to make sure that all this didn't go to his head and make him arrogant. So, Paul says,

To keep me from becoming conceited because of these surpassingly great revelations, there was given me a thorn in my flesh, a messenger of Satan, to torment me. Three times I pleaded with the Lord to take it away from me. But he said to me, "My grace is sufficient for you, for my power is made perfect in weakness." Therefore, I will boast all the more gladly about my weaknesses, so that Christ's power may rest on me (*2 Cor. 12:7-9*).

No one is sure exactly what Paul's thorn in the flesh was. Many people think that this thorn in the flesh may have been some sort of eye affliction (See Gal. 4:15 and 6:11). Regardless of the exact nature of the affliction, several things are clear about how the Apostle Paul sees it:

- Satan was involved. This explains why Paul refers to it as a messenger of Satan.
- It was ultimately sent to Paul, not by Satan, but by God, for a spiritually beneficial purpose. Paul says it was designed to keep him from becoming conceited.
- God heard Paul's prayers asking him to remove it, but God decided not to.

Once again, here in the New Testament, we see a worldview of affliction that is completely consistent with that of Job and the prophets of the Old Testament.

To sum up, the Bible knows nothing of a God who is uninvolved or only marginally involved in sending negative circumstances into people's lives. As far as the Bible is concerned, God makes the final decision about every situation that enters people's lives. God may choose to use intermediate instruments to accomplish those circumstances: other people, weather, even satanic forces. But it is God who personally designs, authorizes and sets limits on every one of the negative circumstances that strikes people's lives. This is the worldview of the Bible.

Therefore, I disagree with Rabbi Kushner's answer to the question, why bad things happen to good people? I believe that the bad things that happen to anybody, happen because Almighty God decides to send those things into people's lives for his own divine purposes.

This is also the answer for that couple in my office. Almighty God decided to send this child into their lives for his own divine purposes.

ALLOWING AFFLICTION VERSUS SENDING AFFLICTION

Now, you may have a bigger problem with the idea of a God who personally afflicted a child with a disability and sent him into these parents' lives than with the idea that God simply allowed this to happen. May I suggest that there really is no difference between the two concepts? If God is truly the sovereign God of the universe as he claims, then what he allows is synonymous with what he sends.

To put it another way, if God decides not to allow some tragedy, it simply doesn't happen. Therefore, if God does decide to allow some tragedy, then by allowing it, God sends it. For all practical purposes, God allowing something and God sending something are identical.

Regardless of the intermediate causes of any given affliction, we must realize that the sovereign controller of all things in the universe is making the final choices.

Even Satan himself has no independent authority in this universe. God orchestrates every circumstance that touches every life to accomplish his perfect purposes. There are no accidents, coincidences, or acts of fate in this world.

It may seem a little like overkill to have spent so much time making this theological point about God's personal role in sending affliction into our lives. But the entire premise of this book rests squarely on this theological position. I believe that there is a high and exalted purpose that explains why God allows heartaches, failures, troubles, and afflictions to enter the lives of godly men and women.

This exalted purpose has nothing to do with consequences for negative behavior or discipline for sin in our lives as Christ-followers. This exalted purpose involves God's deliberate strategy for producing brokenness in the lives of Christ-followers. It is only when we know and believe this that we will be able to embrace the process of brokenness with the peace and surrender that the Lord wants from us. The ultimate answer to this couple's question is this: God has sent this child into your lives for the express purpose of producing spiritual brokenness in you.

WHAT DIFFERENCE DOES THEOLOGY MAKE?

One might be tempted to say that theology is one thing and practical living is another. The reality, however, is that good theology leads to stable and resilient practical living. Nowhere have I found that to be more true than when it comes to the truth of the suffering Brenda and I went through with our daughter Jill. In the early years, the immensity of Jill's disabilities and mental retardation were often overwhelming. Brenda and I nearly gave up. We had hardly any hope in a medical solution, little joy in our lives, and we began to believe there was no way out of the bleak situation we were in. It's difficult to describe the devastation we felt. We could have easily allowed our spiritual lives to lapse into bitterness and cynicism.

What kept up us going and provided a semblance of spiritual and emotional equilibrium was the absolute conviction *theologically* that God was personally involved and connected with all that was happening to us. We decided to believe what God says in the Bible:

- that God was indeed making the final choices about Jill's condition and all that was happening with her;
- that God had a precisely designed plan into which all of this suffering fit perfectly;
- that Jill's condition was not an accident, a coincidence, or an act of random, cruel fate; and
- that God had a high and exalted purpose for all our pain — even though we had no concept of what that might be.

These ideological truths gave us the confidence we needed to press on. They lifted us above our depression and despair and allowed us to go on day after day. Had we not believed these truths, had we decided that God was not in control and our suffering had no redeeming purpose, I'm certain Brenda and I would have collapsed emotionally and psychologically. Our marriage would likely have fallen apart, and our three boys might have grown up to be angry men. And I'm sure that their faith in God, like Brenda's and mine, would have taken a horrible turn for the worse and perhaps disappeared altogether.

These consequences really do happen to people who face enormous suffering. Our family is not some super-family. We're made up of the same protoplasm as every other family. But what kept us together was our family's strong belief in the theological truths described in this chapter. This good and right theology kept us going and gave us the spiritual and emotional equilibrium to withstand the fury. It gave us the resiliency to survive.

If you're facing pain and suffering in your life, then God's got some great theology for you! If you will allow your heart to believe what God says and to trust him, you will discover this wonderful truth found in Isaiah 43:2-4 (excerpted):

When you pass through the waters, I will be with

you; and when you pass through the rivers, they will not sweep over you.

When you walk through the fire, you will not be burned; the flames will not set you ablaze.

For I am the Lord, your God.

FOR DISCUSSION

1. How would you have answered the couple's question before reading the rest of this chapter?
2. As a follower of Christ, what afflictions are you facing that cannot be explained as a consequence of wrong behavior or a discipline for sin in your life?
3. How does it make you feel to say that God sent this affliction in your life?
4. How do you feel about the idea that God sending and God allowing afflictions in our lives is the same thing?
5. Can you accept the idea that affliction, trouble, and even tragedy can have a higher, exalted purpose in people's lives?

Men are God's method.
The church is looking for
better methods;
God is looking for better men...
What the church needs today
is not more machinery or better,
not new organizations
or more novel methods,
but men whom
the Holy Spirit can use...
the Holy Ghost does not come
on machinery, but on men.
He does not anoint plans,
but men.

~E.M. Bounds, *Power Through Prayer*~

CHAPTER TWO

EVERY EXODUS NEEDS A MOSES

It had been a cordial telephone conversation. We were seeking a singles pastor for our church family and I had been speaking with a man who ran a large and successful singles ministry. I had commented that we were looking for God's man with God's anointing to bring God's power to bear on the singles community in our area.

My telephone partner responded with a rebuke of sorts. He urged me to concentrate on getting a coordinated and organized program of ministry going first. That way, he said, the whole ministry would not be so one-man centered.

In response, I said, "Brother, I really appreciate your heart. But I have learned that the key to God's work is always a man or woman of God. Every exodus needs a Moses!"

Ours is a method-oriented world. We Westerners are masters at packaging and exporting methods. We have methods for everything from breathing in childbirth to beating the house at blackjack. And we in the Christian world have clearly been touched by this cultural phenomenon.

We Christ-followers are fanatics, it seems, over successful methods. Let any church or Christian organization carry out something successful in virtually any area of ministry and watch what happens. This group will be besieged by well-intentioned Christians who want to duplicate their methodology. These copycat Christ-followers then set off to implement their imported programs, confident that God's anointing rests upon the method. And when they meet with marginal success at best, they cannot understand what went wrong.

GOD AND METHODOLOGY

When we look at the Bible, we find the explanation. God has put precious little methodology in the Bible. Those of us who have tried in vain to extract a "biblical" method for church management, staff operations, Sunday school organization, or anything else will testify to this. The Bible is remarkably silent in the area of methods.

In pondering this, it occurred to me that nowhere in the Word of God does it say that God anoints a method with his Spirit. God anoints men and women. At Pentecost (Acts 2), it wasn't Peter's sermon that was anointed but Peter. God didn't anoint the Exodus but Moses. It wasn't David's sling that God anointed in the Valley of Elah but David. It wasn't outdoor preaching that God anointed but George Whitefield and John Wesley. The same was true of Deborah and Jonah and Esther and Dwight Moody and Charles G. Finney and Mother Theresa and every other man or woman who has ever shaken this world for Jesus Christ.

That is why God did not give us a list of methods or programs when he provided his plan for successful ministry. Instead, he gave us a list of the qualifications that the men and women who lead his church are to possess. In the Bible, God's focus is on the depth and quality of character that those in Christian leadership must have if the power of God is to be revealed.

Not any man could have accomplished the Exodus — it took Moses. It took a man who had been tempered to a fine spiritual edge with forty years on the back side of the desert; a man who had been with God at the burning bush; a man who knew the ways of God and not just the acts of God. Only such a man could have served as the conduit for God's power as it was displayed in Egypt those many years ago.

In the same way, there could have been no Great Awakening without George Whitefield.

There could have been no missionary journeys

without Paul. There could have been no Reformation without Luther. There could have been no Methodist Revival without Wesley. There could have been no ministry to poor children in India without Mother Theresa.

Men and women are God's method, and any astute observer of human nature and history recognizes this. In the book, *Stonewall Jackson and the American Civil War,* by George F.R. Henderson and Peter Smith, Napoleon is reported to have made this same observation in these words:

> The personality of the general is indispensable. The Gauls were not conquered by the Roman Legions but by Caesar. It was not before the Carthaginian soldiers that Rome was made to tremble but before Hannibal. It was not the Macedonian phalanx which penetrated to India but Alexander.

To this it may be added that it was not the soldiers of the South who stood like a wall between Grant and Richmond but Robert E. Lee. It was not the pilots of the Royal Air Force that stopped Hitler's advance but Winston Churchill.

Men and women are God's method. For every great task, God has always prepared a man or woman first.

THE DILEMMA OF MODERN CHRISTIANITY

Never before in American Christianity has there been a greater need to emphasize this truth.

Media Christianity has begun to threaten the very soul of the church of Jesus Christ. We have begun to associate the moving of God's Spirit with bigness and dazzle and glitter. Theatrics have overshadowed the revival theology of the ancients. Self-promotion has come to be accepted and even applauded among those who purport to be men and women after God's own heart.

Our modern-day brand of Christianity would look very strange indeed to Moses who "regarded disgrace for the sake of Christ of greater value than the treasures of Egypt" (Heb. 11:26). He would tell us sadly that we have forsaken the faith of our fathers to pursue the siren call of Vanity Fair. He would remind us that God was not in the wind or the earthquake or the fire. He would call us back to the theology of anointed, humble, broken men and women of God.

As the twenty-first century American church, we must refocus our thinking. We must resuscitate our understanding of God's principles of revival and spiritual power. We must reject the world system's approach to ministry and spiritual power even though it may be sugar-coated with a few Bible verses. We must begin to seek out and rear up true men and women of God, who understand the ways of God like Moses did. And the ways of God always have, and always will, lead through

brokenness. It is the only pathway for producing powerful, godly men and women.

BROKENNESS IS A NON-NEGOTIABLE

Brokenness is not an optional experience for the person
who desires God to use them in a mighty way. As we
will see in the pages to come, brokenness has been a
critical part of the spiritual preparation process for every
man and woman whose life God has ever used.

To say it another way, you and I as followers of
Christ, cannot and will not see God's anointing and
power manifested through us until brokenness becomes
a reality in our lives. And the more broken we are, the
more of God's anointing and power we will experience.

In teaching about brokenness, I am convinced that
there are greener pastures out there for every Christ-follower. God is no respecter of persons. What the men
and women of God who shook the world in the past
had, can be had by all of us today. God is yearning to
make many of us today into George Whitefields, John
Wesleys, and Mother Theresas. There is spiritual
power for every believer in Jesus Christ.

The portal through which we must pass to secure access to this power is the portal of brokenness.

MY PRAYER AS A YOUNG CHRIST-FOLLOWER

When I gave my life to Jesus in the spring of 1971, I
began praying like this: "Lord, I've lived for the world

and everything in it. I've seen how empty and worthless that is. So now, I want to live for you. I want my life to really count for you. I want you to use me to the max for the glory of Jesus Christ. And whatever it takes for me to be used that way is okay with me. Amen." I know that many followers of Christ have prayed similar prayers.

When I prayed that prayer, I meant it. But the truth is, I had no idea what I was asking for. I had no idea I was asking God to break me and take me down the same path of suffering that every man and woman who had ever prayed a similar prayer had followed.

Frankly, for God to be able to use me as I wanted, I thought all I needed was some theological training in the Bible and some methodological training in Christian work. I honestly believed that spiritual usefulness would be mine if I could simply acquire the right methods to add to my newfound passion for Christ. In fact, I seldom prayed that prayer over the next several years because I was sure I had found the strategy to bring about its fulfillment on my own.

Years later, after I had been to seminary and learned lots about church work, I was surprised and disappointed to discover that God was still not using me as I had asked him to so many years before. What's worse, I was out of strategies to get there. So I went back to God, frustrated and confused, and began praying the simple little prayer from my spiritual infancy. But this time it was different. I ended with a new sentence: "Lord, I can't get myself to this place of spiritual usefulness, so you need to get me there."

What I didn't know at that point is what we have talked about in this chapter. I still thought usefulness to Christ was all about methods and knowledge and human experience. I knew nothing about needing God's Spirit to flow through me unhindered. I didn't realize that spiritual usefulness is all about spiritual formation in my own heart. I was ignorant of the process by which God prepares his servants.

Still, I was sincere in my prayer. And knowing that, God set out to answer it in a way I never would have expected. In 1992, he sent Jill into my life. She was a central piece in God's plan to answer my prayer. I see this so clearly now. Unfortunately, as Jill's disabilities began to take me down a road of pain and suffering, I failed to make the spiritual connection.

It seemed to me that rather than rewarding me for asking God to use my life, God was somehow punishing me. The whole thing baffled me. It seemed so nonsensical, so contrary to human logic: volunteer for God to use you and instead he curses you.

Maybe you can relate. Maybe you have prayed a prayer like mine and it seems like God has abused and deserted you in response. You asked for greener pastures and God sent you to the backside of the desert instead.

Don't fret. God is simply preparing you so that he can use you the way you asked him to.

The preparation is nasty, but it's a necessary part of God's answer to our prayer. Nobody likes, wants, or understands these early steps. I certainly didn't. But here is the good news. At the end of the tunnel there is a great light – the light of spiritual power and anointing, of usefulness to God and spiritual impact for Christ on our world.

Like all of God's servants, I had to learn this lesson the hard way. I won't lie and say it was easy. I often wondered why I had ever prayed that prayer. Many days I told God that I had decided to revoke my prayer because I didn't think I'd survive the process needed to answer it. But God knew my heart. He knew that more than anything, I wanted my life to count for Christ. Because of that, God ignored my complaints and kept going.

Almost thirteen years later, I'm still standing, thanks to God's amazing grace. During this time, I've seen God answer my prayer in greater and greater measure. As I look back, I'm thankful I didn't bail out on the process. I'd never want to endure it again, but I'm honestly glad God put me through it. The release of his Spirit in my life was well worth it.

Here is the bottom line: God will use your life for his glory if that's your true desire — but it will cost you something. Don't forget what Paul said in 2 Timothy

2:20-21: "In a large house, there are articles not only of gold and silver, but also of wood and clay; some for noble purposes and some for ignoble. If a man cleanses himself from the latter (which as we'll see is what the process of brokenness is all about), he will be an instrument for noble purposes, made holy, useful to the Master and prepared to do any good work."

My hope is that, in your heart, the end that Paul describes here will be worth the means.

FOR DISCUSSION

1. Do you agree that the work of God today has become too dependent on methods? Why or why not?
2. Do you agree that men and women are God's method? Why or why not?
3. Why do you think that the modern-day church tends to focus more on methodology than on developing men and women of God?
4. If brokenness is really essential for a person to experience God's power in their life, then are you prepared to ask God for this experience in your life, regardless of what it may cost? Why or why not?

When God wants to do an impossible task,
He takes an impossible individual —
and crushes him.

~Dr. Alan Redpath, *The Making of a Man of God*~

CHAPTER THREE

REDUCING OUR RESISTANCE

The famous Chinese protégé of Hudson Taylor, Watchman Nee, said in his book, *The Normal Christian Life,* "Anyone who serves God will discover sooner or later that the greatest hindrance to his work is not others, but himself."

One of the most significant days in the life of any follower of Jesus Christ is the day when he or she realizes that the greatest obstacle they have to ministering with power for Jesus Christ is themselves: their self-life, self-reliance, self-dependence, self-trust, self-sufficiency, self-love, and self-wisdom.

These are the great barriers to seeing the supernatural power of God flow through our lives. These are the things that quench and grieve the Holy Spirit and rob us of his free-flowing power.

God has a solution for our problem. His solution is brokenness. The concept of brokenness is one of the most beautiful and precious in all of the Word of God. It is also one of the most vital if a Christ-follower wants to know and experience the power of Almighty God.

One of the most effective ways to get a grasp on brokenness is to see it displayed in the life of biblical characters. Since Moses is one of the greatest examples of brokenness in all of the Word of God, his life will serve as our living classroom on brokenness. So let's look at what God does with him in order to get some insight into what brokenness is.

THE EXAMPLE OF MOSES

Most people are somewhat familiar with Moses' early life in Egypt as told in the first two chapters of the Book of Exodus: how he was cast adrift in the Nile by his mother in order to save him from Pharaoh's edict (Exod. 1:16); how he was found by Pharaoh's daughter (Exod. 2:6); how he was called her son and raised in Pharaoh's house for forty years (Exod. 2:10).

The Bible is silent regarding the events of Moses's first forty years in the palace of Egypt. However, the historian, Flavius Josephus, provides us with some ancient tradition about Moses's life during those years.

In *The Antiquities of the Jews* (Book II, Chapter 10) Josephus records that when Moses was a young man in the court of Pharaoh, the Ethiopians invaded

Egypt from the south and succeeded in occupying a significant portion of the country. Pharaoh asked Moses to assume command of the army of Egypt and to meet the Ethiopians in battle. Moses agreed and, by a marvelous strategy, surprised the Ethiopian army and routed them. Moses then pursued the Ethiopians into their own land and conquered their capital city, thus ending the threat to Egypt. Moses returned home to great glory and honor.

Josephus implies that these events established Moses as a national hero and positioned him to become a man of great power and influence in the political world of Egypt. His star was on the rise in Egypt and everyone knew it.

This came to a screeching halt, however, when Moses decided to take an interest in the oppressed Israelites. His aborted attempt at being their savior (Exod. 2:11-14) resulted in his killing an Egyptian citizen, an act that was certain to arouse the anger of Pharaoh against him. This caused him to flee Egypt and head into the Sinai wilderness — the "far side of the desert," as Exodus. 3:1 calls it.

In an instant, Moses went from national hero to fugitive. All that he had worked for in terms of human power and position dissolved around him in a few short days. Now, why did God let this happen to Moses? Well, the Bible gives us insight. Hebrews 11:27a says, "By faith he left Egypt not fearing the king's anger..."

In Hebrews 11, God gives us a fascinating commentary on the events that radically altered Moses's life at age forty. God tells us that Moses's reason for leaving Egypt was not that he was afraid of Pharaoh's displeasure. In fact, it is quite possible that Moses could have made peace with Pharaoh and been allowed to remain in Egypt had he humbled himself, or at least made an attempt to do so.

But, apparently, Moses did not even try to patch things up with Pharaoh. You see, Moses had made a momentous decision. He had decided that he did not care about what Egypt had to offer him. Instead, he had decided that he wanted to serve God. He wanted to spend his life earning rewards in heaven. Remember what Hebrews 11 says: "He regarded disgrace for the sake of Christ as of greater value than the treasures of Egypt, because he was looking ahead to his reward" (Heb. 11:26).

This is why he had gone out to visit his people, the Israelites, and tried to help them. His attempt was a clumsy effort at serving God and it was an indication of where his heart had come to be.

In response to Moses's sincere desire to turn away from the treasures of Egypt and devote his life to serving God, what did God do? God permitted Moses to be driven from Egypt. This may not seem like it makes sense, but it does. Let me explain.

God was pleased with Moses's choice. God is excited when any man or woman decides to forego the trinkets of this world in exchange for him. But God also knows that no man or woman — not even Moses — can serve God without brokenness.

So God sent Moses out into the Sinai desert to prepare Moses for the very objective to which Moses had now dedicated his life: becoming a servant of the living God. For such a calling, Moses needed to be broken.

As contrary as it might seem to our human logic, God's plan to take Moses down on the human level in response to his desire to serve God makes perfect sense on the spiritual level. In God's economy, the way up is the way down. In God's service, brokenness always precedes true usefulness. If we fail to grasp this truth, we will often be confused by the way God is directing our lives as Christ-followers.

As Moses entered the Sinai desert alone, he was no doubt confused. Perhaps he was even afraid. The ancient area of Sinai was arid steppeland inhabited by nomads who grazed their flocks of sheep and goats there. After the pomp and splendor of Egypt, this must have seemed like the most desolate and unfriendly place in the world to Moses. Moses must have wondered why God would do this to him after he had made such an impressive and life-changing choice to put God first in his life.

Moses spent forty years in Sinai, lost from sight to the civilized world that swirled around the Nile. The

Bible is strangely silent about all that happened to Moses during those forty years. Although the Bible doesn't record the details, there was a marvelous spiritual process that God worked inside Moses on the backside of the desert — a process that would eventually allow Moses to fulfill the very destiny to which he had committed himself forty years before.

The point is that when Moses emerged from his forty years on the backside of the desert, he was a totally different man. During these forty years, God spiritually broke Moses.

BEFORE AND AFTER BROKENNESS

Watchman Nee was one of the first to write about how God broke Moses. Charles Stanley followed Nee's work. So let's build on their contributions and take another look at Moses's life before and after these forty years. It will give us a good idea of what brokenness really looks like. Exodus 2 describes a number of Moses's qualities before he spent his time in Sinai. He was:

- *Self-confident*
  In Exodus 2, Moses was sure that he could handle the job of leading Israel out of Egypt. He had all the education, leadership skills, training, and wisdom that Egypt could give a man, and he trusted in it.

- *Self-assured*

  In Exodus 2, Moses was sure that he could meet the demands of serving God in his own energy and strength. It never occurred to Moses that there might be anything he couldn't do if he set his mind to it.

- *Self-sufficient*

  In Exodus 2, not once does the Bible tell of Moses relying on God to help him pull off this "exodus" of his own. Moses's sufficiency is found in himself exclusively.

- *Self-wise*

  In Exodus 2, Moses trusted his own logic and wisdom to deal with problems and people. He analyzed the Hebrews' situation and devised his own plan to resolve things. Trusting the supernatural power and wisdom of God to solve problems was an approach totally unfamiliar to Moses.

- *Self-willed*

  In Exodus 2, Moses knew nothing of waiting on God. He had his own agenda in life. Even his best intentions of helping the Israelites were contaminated by his fleshly impulsiveness. He knew nothing of prayer and seeking God and waiting on God's timing. "Be still and know that I am God" (Ps. 46:10) was simply not a part of Moses's methodology.

Clearly, Moses knew nothing of the ways of God at age forty. He was wise in the wisdom of the world, which is foolishness to God. He was a mighty man, but he relied upon his own human strength and ability instead of God's. He had leadership skills, but they were rooted in the impulsive ways of the flesh. He had the right objective in mind, but he knew nothing of waiting on God's timing and plan to accomplish it.

It's true that God had important work for Moses to do. But Moses at age forty was not yet equipped. He had been to the University of Egypt and had learned well in the school of man. But God knew that Moses needed to attend the school of God.

So God sent Moses out into the desert to attend Wilderness Theological Seminary where the only faculty member is God himself; the classes meet on the backside of the desert; the one degree offered is a Ph.D. in the ways of God; and the length of study is as long as it takes for the lessons to be learned. In Moses' case, this was forty years. When he graduated, Moses was not the same man.

This change in Moses is quite clear when one compares the Moses of Exodus chapter 2 with the Moses of Exodus chapter 3:

- Moses is still educated, but that education has been tempered by the ways of God.
- Gone is the self-assurance and self-reliance of forty years earlier.
- Gone is the haughty self-sufficiency so obvious forty years before. Now, Moses feels totally inadequate for the very same task that he was so sure he could accomplish forty years earlier. Moses said this to God at the burning bush: "Who am I, that I should go to Pharaoh and bring the Israelites out of Egypt?" (Exod. 3:11).
- Gone is the impetuous, fleshly zeal that knew nothing of waiting on God. In its place is an active resting in God to do God's work, God's way, in God's time, by God's power.

The man that we see in Exodus 3 is not the same man who went into the desert a generation before. This radical change was displayed when Moses spoke to the Hebrew people just before God parted the Red Sea: "Moses answered the people, 'Do not be afraid. Stand firm and you will see the deliverance the Lord will bring today. The Egyptians you see today you will never see again. The Lord will fight for you, you need only to be still'" (Exod. 14:13-14).

What we have in Moses over these forty years in Sinai is an awesome, revolutionary, all-consuming, spiritual transformation! And now, Moses was useable to

God. Now the vessel had been prepared for the Master's use.

How did God transform Moses from a well-meaning man into a powerful and effective servant of God? The answer is that he broke Moses of his self-life. He broke him of the self-trust, the self-assurance, the self-sufficiency, the self-wisdom, and the self-will that characterized his life during his first forty years. In their place, God substituted trust, reliance, wisdom, and strength that was rooted solely in God himself.

How did God break Moses? As Stanley suggests, it was by stripping away from Moses all the things he had considered so valuable in his early life. God took away his fame, fortune, power, influence, and prestige. God sent Moses out into the desert and made him a nobody. God took Moses down to bedrock. God pulled all of the props out from under him. God forced Moses to learn what it means to depend on God plus nothing for every single aspect of his life. This is what brokenness is all about.

BROKENNESS DEFINED

After observing Moses, a working definition of brokenness is now possible. Brokenness is the process by which God dislodges our self-life and teaches us to rely upon him alone in every facet of our lives. Brokenness is the process whereby God crushes all our self-dependence and, in its place, substitutes an utter dependence on God and God alone in every area of our lives.

Through brokenness, God replaces:

- our self-sufficiency with a dependence on the sufficiency of God;
- our self-reliance with a reliance on God alone;
- our self-wisdom with a wisdom rooted in the ways and word of God; and
- our self-will with a surrender to the will and timing and plan of God, tempering our human zeal with a deep waiting upon God.

The purpose of this whole process is to make us more useable to Almighty God.

Brokenness may be a new spiritual concept for many of us, so let's take an example from the physical world to further our understanding. As we all know, electricity flows through wires. How freely it flows is directly proportional to the amount of resistance that the wire offers. The greater the wire's resistance, the more it hinders the flow of electrical power.

This physical principle, which we all understand so well, provides a picture of what spiritual brokenness is all about. If we picture ourselves as the wire and the supernatural power of God as the electricity, then, we understand that God's power flows best through wires with the least resistance.

The goal, then, of spiritual brokenness is to reduce

a Christ-follower's resistance to the flow of God's Spirit through his or her life. This helps us understand why God must break us in order to use us.

Our self-life and all of its out-workings — self-trust, self-reliance, self-wisdom, self-will — are the things that increase our resistance to the Holy Spirit's movement in and through our lives. These things grieve the Spirit and limit our usefulness for Christ. These aspects of our self-life clog up the our spiritual pipes and restrict the free flow of God's power through our lives.

The bottom line is this: spiritual usefulness without spiritual brokenness is a spiritual impossibility.

IS BROKENNESS REALLY SO IMPORTANT?

At this point, one might ask: is brokenness really such a major issue with God? Let's allow Jesus himself to respond to that question. In John 12:23-26, Jesus is in Jerusalem and only several days away from the cross. In fact, Jesus says these words on the very heels of riding down the Mount of Olives on a donkey and entering the city to the shouts of hosanna in the event commonly called the Triumphal Entry (John 12:12-19).

Instead of immediately speaking to his disciples about all the glory, pomp, and pageantry that they have just experienced, Jesus talks to them about brokenness. He says, "I tell you the truth, unless a kernel of wheat falls to the ground and dies, it remains only a single seed. But if it dies, it produces many seeds" (John 12:24).

Although many Christian commentators have struggled to interpret what Jesus really means in this passage, Watchman Nee has grasped the Lord's point perfectly. In Nee's explanation, Jesus draws on truth from the physical world to teach truth about the spiritual world. A kernel of wheat with its hard outer shell intact is useless. The wheat cannot sprout and grow. There is life on the inside, but it cannot be released. However, when the wheat's hard outer shell is broken and cracked open, then the life of the wheat can come out and grow and bear fruit and bring blessing to its world.

The real issue is not whether there is life inside the kernel of wheat but whether the life that is inside can get out and make an impact on the world around it. And this depends on whether its hard outer shell has been broken.

Jesus points to this truth of nature and declares that it is the secret to bringing forth "many seeds" for God. So, Jesus says, a Christ-follower is just like a kernel of wheat. When we give our lives to Christ, the Holy Spirit takes up residence in our innermost being. Just like the kernel of wheat, we have the spiritual life inside of us.

But every one of us still has that hard outer shell of our self-life. The result is that the life and power of the Spirit of God can't get out — it can't flow through us. Just like physical seeds, God must break the hard outer shell of every Christ-follower so that the life of God can pulsate through us freely and spill out onto the world around us.

Since bringing forth fruit for God should be a normal part of every Christ-follower's life, and since Jesus directs us to brokenness as the source of all fruitfulness for God, we have no choice but to conclude that brokenness is a strategic issue for every believer in Jesus Christ. In fact, I would go so far as to say that brokenness is *the* basic issue for every Christ-follower who wants to live for God, serve God, and make a serious impact on the world for Jesus Christ. Indeed, the biographies of all the great men and women of God reveal that this was the one central issue with which, sooner or later, every one of them had to come to grips.

ISN'T THERE AN EASIER WAY?

Since the process of brokenness is tough and painful, this is a fair question. Once again, let's allow Jesus himself to answer it. In John 15:5, Jesus said, "I am the vine; you are the branches. If a man remains in me and I in him, he will bear much fruit; apart from me you can do nothing."

We all recognize that a branch can only bear fruit when it is experiencing the vine's free flow of sap. Christ uses this botanical truth to teach spiritual truth, declaring that, in the same way, we as followers of Christ can bear fruit only when we have the free flow of the sap of the Spirit through our lives.

Jesus repeated this same spiritual truth to his disciples while he was teaching in the synagogue at Capernaum. "The Spirit gives life; the flesh counts nothing" (John 6:63a). Jesus says that it is the Holy Spirit who imparts life and power and ministry and fruit — our fleshly efforts can produce nothing of lasting spiritual value or impact.

If this is so — and Jesus says that it is — then brokenness is an unavoidable portal through which we must pass if we are to see the power of God manifested in and through our lives. For as we have already seen, brokenness is the key to experiencing the sap of God's Spirit flowing freely in our lives. We cannot go around brokenness or avoid it altogether because it is the one and only pathway to maximum blessing, fruitfulness and anointing from God.

Many Christ-followers believe they will have power from God because they have learned the Bible and systematic theology well. Tragically, they imagine that if they could simply get a little more Bible teaching or accumulate a few more Bible facts or memorize a few more verses or attend a few more seminars, then suddenly they would erupt with the power of God. But this is simply not so.

Studying the Bible is not a bad thing, nor is it to be in any way discouraged. But Bible knowledge in itself is not the secret to fruitfulness for God. The key to fruitfulness is the free flow of the Holy Spirit and his power through our lives.

If we are ever going to be of any useful service to God as Christ-followers, all of us must come to grips with this eternal truth. No matter how many people we can impress with our cleverness or attract with our personality or influence by our persuasive words or motivate with our natural abilities — spiritually, the results come to nothing! It's all flesh.

This was the hard lesson that Moses learned so painfully in Exodus chapter 2. And so many followers of Christ — after passing through much frustration and failure in trying to serve God just as Moses did — have ended up right back here at Jesus's words: "The Spirit gives life; the flesh counts for nothing" (John 6:63a).

This is an immutable, eternal, unchanging law of God. A person either complies with it or they don't, but God doesn't alter it for anyone. That is why brokenness is such an important issue: it is the only way to have the power of God crown our life and to be seriously fruitful for the kingdom of God.

BROKENNESS AND USEFULNESS TO GOD

At this point you may very well ask, are you saying that I cannot be used by God at all unless I'm broken? The answer is that no one is ever fully broken. No

Christ-follower ever reaches the point of zero resistance. Brokenness is an ongoing, lifelong process.

But it's true that the more broken we are, the more God can and will use us. Brokenness and usefulness are directly proportional. To the degree that a Christ-follower is unbroken, to that same degree God cannot really use him or her for true Spirit-empowered ministry. That Christ-follower can perform a lot of activity around the church, but it's all just the energy of the flesh. It is simply wood, hay and straw in God's sight. That person is exactly where Moses was at age forty. And as we have seen, God had to break him to use him.

You may also wonder whether you should give up what you're presently doing for Jesus until you get to be more broken. The answer is: absolutely not. God may set you aside for a time, but setting yourself aside in your own human wisdom is the worst thing you could ever do. Instead, keep serving the Lord with all your sincere effort and begin asking God to make you ever more broken as you do.

THE EXAMPLE OF D.L. MOODY

In 1871, Moody was serving as the director of the YMCA in Chicago. Moody would preach every Sunday to crowds of over a thousand people in Chicago's Farwell Hall. He had served on numerous committees, taught Sunday School, started mission churches, been a chaplain to the Union Army, and worked the slums of

Chicago for Christ. He had even been sought after to run for Congress.

If anyone could have brought in the kingdom of God by sheer output of energy, Moody could have. In fact, his zeal was so unbounded that even his admirers often referred to him as Crazy Moody.

But there was something wrong. Moody was participating in a wealth of activity, but his ministry lacked the demonstration of the Spirit and power. Two older women noticed this and began to pray for him. In *The Life of Dwight L. Moody*, a book by his son, the women would attend his meetings during the summer and sit in the front row. While Moody preached, they prayed. At the close of the services they would approach him and say, "We have been praying for you."

"Why don't you pray for these people?" Moody would ask indignantly.

"Because you need the power of the Spirit," they would say.

"I need power?" Moody would puff in disbelief.

At first, Moody dismissed these two ladies. "Why, I thought I had power," Moody said years later. "I had the largest congregations in Chicago, and there were many conversions. I was in a sense satisfied. But right along those two women kept praying for me, and their earnest talk about anointing for special service set me thinking.... There came a great hunger in my soul. I did not know what it was. I began to cry out as I never did before. I really felt that I did not want to live if I could not have this power for service."

By the time October 1871 came, Moody was openly admitting his need for God to break him and begging God to give him power from on high. In response, God burned down the YMCA building in Chicago. God also burned down Farwell Hall, the other churches where Moody preached, Moody's offices — even Moody's house. In fact, God burned down the entire city of Chicago!

Moody lost all his belongings. All that he had labored for fifteen years to build for Jesus went up in smoke in the Great Chicago Fire. Finally, Moody found himself in New York City, alone in a small room, devastated. But his spiritual hunger remained.

Here, God brought Moody to the end of himself. Here, Moody suddenly saw how much of his work in Chicago had been propelled by his own energy, power, and drive. Here, Moody confessed that he had been like Moses in the early years of Moses's life.

Here, with all the props knocked out from under him, Moody saw the utter futility of all his human energy and effort. He saw how much of his ministry in Chicago had been the result of "zeal without knowledge" (as he put it). Here, Moody repudiated his self-life and its domination of the work of the ministry.

Here, quietly, Moody surrendered himself totally to God.

God had brought D. L. Moody to the end of himself. It had been a long and painful experience, but God had finally broken D. L. Moody. Now the dead, dry days were gone. "Before this, I was always tugging and carrying the water myself," Moody said. "Now I have a river that carries me!"

That river was the power of the Spirit of God, released and free to flow in Moody's life. And Crazy Moody became "Broken Moody, the Man of God," who went on to shake two continents for Jesus Christ.

How beautiful and how powerful is the believer who has been broken by God. Stubbornness and self-love have given way to the sweet fragrance of God in that life. The power of Almighty God radiates from that life.

Brokenness is not a curse. It is a blessing that every follower of Christ needs desperately. Perhaps the fact that it is so seldom spoken of in modern Christianity helps explain why our modern brand of Christianity is so insipid and powerless.

Each one of us needs God to do to us what he did to Moses and to thousands like him whose lives have made an impact on this world for Jesus Christ. Brokenness is a biblical principle for every Christ-follower. It's a principle for you.

MY DREAMS AND MOTIVES

When I first came to McLean Bible Church in 1980 as

the senior pastor, I was not all that senior. In fact, at thirty –years old, I was pretty green. But I had a dream, and it was to see McLean Bible become a large and influential church in the nation's capital — for it to become a household word in the world's most powerful city.

The problem was not with my dream but with the motive behind it. I was like Moses in Exodus 2. I had the right idea but the wrong reason. This was not evident to me during the early 1980s, but it was obvious to some members of my congregation. There was one woman in particular who would write me notes from time to time. She was a bit like the two women who prayed for Dwight L. Moody. She would tell me about my arrogance, my self-wisdom, and my self-dependence. She constantly rebuked me for glorifying myself instead of Christ. And she called on me to acknowledge these self-sins as hindrances to the flow of God's power in my life and in the life of our church.

Frankly, this lady's notes irritated the dickens out of me. As such, it was easy to write her off and view her assessment of my life as flat-out wrong. I saw no arrogance, fleshly pride, or self-dependence. I was certain I was not out for my own glory.

At the same time, however, I had a nagging feeling that maybe she was on to something. McLean Bible was not growing or making the impact I dreamed it would. Something *was* wrong, but I couldn't put my finger on what it was. I was working hard, studying diligently, preparing my messages carefully, preaching them fervently, and leading the church faithfully.

Even so, what I had yet to come to grips with was John 6:63: "The Spirit gives life; the flesh counts for nothing." My flesh was working hard, but what I needed was God's Spirit to begin moving through me with power. And so, much like Moody, I began asking God to change things. I didn't realize it at the time, but what I was really asking for was brokenness. I now look on this time as one of the greatest turning points in my life as a servant of Jesus Christ.

So what did God do? First, he sent so much internal church strife and conflict my way that, by the late 1980s, my nerves were stretched to the breaking point. When this was resolved favorably in 1991, I was sure I was where the Lord needed me to be in terms of brokenness. But I was wrong — in a big way. In January 1992, my daughter Jill was born and I found out how mistaken I was. By July, she was having hundreds of seizures a month and Brenda and I were starting to slide into a black hole of despondency. Personally, I was entering the deepest part of my *backside of the desert* experience.

God used this pain and helplessness to do to me what he did to Moses in the forty years between Exodus 1 and 2. He used it to strip away all my self-resourcefulness, self-wisdom, and self-sufficiency. He used it to shatter my self-will, my fleshly self-reliance, and my self-assurance.

It took several years of intense suffering until I reached the place where I no longer cared about how many people showed up for church. I no longer worried about becoming a big shot with a reputation among the saints. All I cared about was that Jesus himself received the credit and the spotlight, no matter how many people were around to be a part of it. I can't explain exactly how God produced these changes. But regardless of God's mechanism, the result was profound.

Success could never have refined me like this – and God knew it. He produced these changes in the intense furnace of suffering and pain. God used Jill's disability to bring me to the end of myself.

Looking back now, I can say without reservation that I needed to be broken. The lady who wrote me those letters was right, but I couldn't see it. It's clear to me now that there was no way God could use my life or bless my service for him in my unbroken condition. Guess what happened? The less I cared about how many people showed up at church, the more people came. The less I cared how influential McLean Bible Church was, the more influential it became. The more I tried to exalt Jesus and turn the spotlight on him, the more the media spotlight turned on my activities in leading the church. While these may have increased my profile, the exaltation of self is simply not a consideration. It's all about uplifting the Lord Jesus and spreading the Good News of his offer of eternal life.

I can't explain the exact dynamics of this change. But I do know that what was once a perilous threat to my soul no longer is. Because of this, I believe God now feels he can send some things to me and McLean Bible Church that he could never have sent years ago – before Jill and before brokenness.

This is the lesson of brokenness. God *will* send success, but he first must send failure, tragedy, and or other ills to push us to the end of our strength. This is the path that leads to success and a fuller life and service for Christ. Our evil, wiggling self-life must be crushed so that our only motive is to exalt Christ and our only strategy for doing it is John 6:63. There is no other way and God makes no exceptions.

DISCUSSION POINTS

1. Do you agree with the idea that the greatest hindrance to our serving God is ourselves? How does this ring true in your own life?
2. How are you similar to the Moses we see in Exodus 2?
3. Review the definitions of *brokenness* given in this chapter. Rate your current level of brokenness (0-100 percent) on this definition.

4. How do you feel about the statement: spiritual usefulness without spiritual brokenness is impossible?
5. Do you agree that brokenness is a strategic issue for your life?
6. Do you yearn for spiritual power in your life to such a degree that you're willing to ask God for brokenness? What are some of the fears that might be holding you back?

We thank thee, Lord, for pilgrim days
When dusty springs were dry,
When first we knew what depths of need,
Thy love could satisfy.

~Hudson Taylor's Spiritual Secret~

CHAPTER FOUR

EMBRACING THE PRODUCT, RESISTING THE PROCESS

A great man of God was once asked by a friend how he learned to make so many good decisions. "By making so many bad decisions!" he said in reply. Indeed, experience *is* the best teacher.

As Charles Stanley points out, the trouble with us as human beings is that we all want the product, but we don't want the process. Everybody wants to have the wisdom to make good decisions, but nobody wants to go through the process of making the bad decisions that it takes to get there. Everybody wants to be a great athlete, but nobody wants to go through the off-the-field discipline that it takes to get there.

The very same thing is true when it comes to brokenness. As Christ-followers, we can see the great benefits of being broken but we recoil at the process that it takes to get us there. We know that God never uses success to break anybody. The process that leads to brokenness is bloody and painful and heart-wrenching. And the only reason that anyone would seek it is that they are convinced that the product is worth it.

In the previous chapter, we saw how God broke D.L. Moody. It was a difficult and agonizing process that God put Moody through. But listen to what Moody said in *The Life of Dwight L. Moody* after it was over: "I went to preaching again. The sermons were not different. I did not present any new truths and yet now thousands were converted...I would not now be placed back where I was before if you were to give me the world...It would be as the small dust of the balance."

Moody discovered that the process that leads to brokenness is painful but the product is more than worth it.

No one regrets being broken, because on the other side of brokenness lies new intimacy with God and new power to serve him. However, no one who has been through the process would dare say it was easy or that they ever wanted to go through it again.

In this chapter, we will examine the process that God uses to break us. Understanding this process will liberate many Christ-followers who are in the middle of being broken by God and don't understand what is happening to them. We need to be able to properly interpret what God is doing our lives. So much of our past and present life only makes sense when we understand the process of Brokenness.

GOD'S TECHNIQUE

"The Lord employs two different ways to break our outward man," Watchman Nee said in the *Release of the Spirit*. "One is gradual, the other sudden." Neither of these techniques is mutually exclusive. God uses them in concert with one another to accomplish his work of breaking.

The first technique we'll discuss is the ongoing, lifelong process. No one is ever fully broken. No one ever reaches zero resistance. So God employs a gradual, ongoing process of trials and struggles to deepen and enhance our brokenness. And this process continues throughout our lives.

There is a second technique, however. Even though brokenness is a lifelong process, God's plan of brokenness always calls for at least one bedrock, shattering experience for every Christ-follower. This is an experience like God gave Moses in Exodus 2 and 3.

This shattering experience is the part that normally comes first chronologically and sets the whole process of brokenness in motion. It is also the part that people remember all their lives. It is the part that people most fear before it happens and thank God for once it is over because they are living with the blessed results of it.

What kind of experience is this bedrock, shattering

experience? It is an experience that knocks every single human prop out from under us. It can be a sudden experience like the loss of a loved one or some other terrible tragedy. It can be a more lengthy experience like a chronic illness or an ongoing series of human defeats and failures.

It is an experience that brings us to the utter end of ourselves. It is an experience where God shatters our self-reliance and self-sufficiency and self-resourcefulness with one mighty blow. Through such an experience God forever alters our view of self, God, life, and ministry.

In this experience God delivers the one crushing blow needed to split open a person's hard outer shell like Jesus talks about in John 12. It is after this has been done — and only after this has been done — that God can put in motion the more gentle, gradual, and lifelong part of the process.

For every follower of Christ, this bedrock experience has a unique character. This has led many to ask: how will I know for certain when God has delivered such a blow to me? The answer to this is quite simple: when God does this to you, believe me, you will know it.

BEDROCK EXPERIENCES IN THE BIBLE

In order to prove that this bedrock experience is really a valid biblical principle, let's examine some biblical examples of it in action.

Moses

Moses's utter failure in Exodus 2 and his forty-year wilderness experience as a nobody on the backside of the desert was God's shattering blow to his life. Out of this experience Moses emerges in Exodus chapter 3 at the burning bush as a transformed man with a transformed view of himself, God, and serving God. In the place of self-sufficiency, there is now inadequacy. In the place of arrogance, there is now the fear of God. In the place of fleshly haste, there is waiting on God. Moses is not a fully broken man, but the shattering blow has been delivered and the rest of Moses's life now becomes a chronicle of God's deepening and maturing this man's brokenness.

Peter

In Matthew 26:33, 35, Peter defiantly declared to Jesus: "Even if all fall away on account of you, I never will. Even if I have to die with you, I will never disown you." What courage! What loyalty! In Luke 22:54-62, we find out how well Peter was able to follow through on his words. Here, Peter denies Jesus three times even as Jesus had predicted he would. "The Lord turned and looked straight at Peter. Then Peter remembered the words the Lord had spoken to him: 'Before the rooster crows today, you will disown me three times.' And he went outside and wept bitterly" (Luke 22:61-62).

In one fell swoop, God shattered this proud, burly

fisherman. In fact, Peter was so thoroughly crushed that he abandoned the ministry altogether. John 21 tells us that he went back to fishing until the risen Lord went and called him back into serving Christ. However, look at the Peter we find in the Book of Acts. He has the same bold and outspoken personality, but noticeably absent are all the self-sins that so characterized him in the Gospels. In their place is the free-flowing, pulsating power of the Spirit of God. Peter was not totally broken of all self-life (Gal. 2:11). But God had delivered the knock-down blow to Peter that sent him down the road of brokenness and usefulness to God for the rest of his life.

Jacob

Although Jacob was destined to play a major role in God's plan for the Hebrew people, his early life was characterized by unbridled self-life. He was a man of deception, scheming, and manipulation. He was a worldly opportunist who craftily maneuvered his brother, Esau, out of his birthright (Gen. 25) and flat out stole his brother's blessing (Gen. 27). We see the same kind of operational style at work in Jacob in Genesis 30 where he engineered the manipulation of speckled and spotted sheep within his father-in-law Laban's flock for his own profit. But God had a divine appointment with brokenness for Jacob. This appointment occurred at the ford of the Jabbok River (Gen. 32:22).

In obedience to God, Jacob returned to Canaan some twenty years after fleeing in fear of his brother Esau. His servants informed him that Esau was coming to meet him with four-hundred armed men. Expecting to meet Esau on the next day, Jacob settled down to spend the night alone at the Jabbok River. He was full of fear and apprehension at the next day's events. His attempts to appease Esau's anger seemed to have failed. He had no armed men with which to defend himself and his family. There, on the lonely banks of the Jabbok, Jacob finally came to the end of his fleshly resourcefulness. The wrestling match between Jacob and the angel that took place all night was merely an outward picture of the struggle that was going on in Jacob's soul. It was a struggle over the issue of full surrender to God and full dependence on God rather than self. After struggling all night, Jacob lost the outward wrestling match, indicating that he had also capitulated inwardly. As a result, God touched Jacob's thigh and Jacob limped for the rest of his life, an ever-present reminder of his brokenness experience.

Jacob won by losing. Up to this point, the Bible never once records the phrase *and God blessed him* in reference to Jacob. Yet, right after his loss at Jabbok, in Genesis 32:29 we find the words: "Then he (God) blessed him (Jacob) there" [parenthesis mine]. And we find this same phrase, *God blessed Jacob*, appearing regularly from this point on in the book of Genesis. In fact, so pervasive was the change in Jacob that God even changed his name to Israel as an outward sign of this change. Jacob was never the same again. Never again do we find him repeating the unspiritual tactics so characteristic of him before his bedrock brokenness experience here at the Jabbok River.

J. Sidlow Baxter, the great Bible commentator, said in his book, *Explore the Book*, "What happened at lonely Jabbok was a critical divine encounter to save this man from himself. The Jabbok wrestling match was meant to crush a wiggling something that had always been in Jacob's nature. Jacob the supplanter needed himself to be supplanted! Yet the wrestling match which crippled him, crowned him — as indicated in the God-given change of his name: Israel, a Prince with God."

Additional Examples

To those already discussed, we can add a host of additional biblical examples:

- God delivered the shattering blow to Job when he let Satan destroy Job's family, possessions, and health.
- God delivered the shattering blow to David when he allowed King Saul to chase David around as a fugitive in the Judean wilderness for seven years.
- God delivered the shattering blow to the prophet Isaiah when God gave him the vision of God's

holiness in Isaiah 6, utterly devastating the prophet's own self-righteousness.

- God delivered the shattering blow to Abraham when he asked Abraham to sacrifice his most precious possession in the world, his son Isaac.
- God delivered the shattering blow to Joseph when he let Joseph be sold into slavery and then be humiliated and incarcerated for thirteen years despite Joseph's innocence.
- God delivered the shattering blow to Apostle Paul when He led him out into the Arabian desert for three years of spiritual preparation and humiliation.

Furthermore, as we look down the corridors of time since the Bible was written, we find that God has sent such a shattering experience into the life of every great man and woman of God.

- Martin Luther's shattering experience was his year of hiding and rejection in the Castle of Wartburg.
- John Wesley's shattering experience was his abysmal failure as a missionary in the colony of Georgia.
- Fanny Crosby's shattering experience was her blindness caused in infancy by improper treatment carried out by a quack doctor. Yet, according to her biographer, Bernard Ruffin, four days

before she died, Fanny said, "I believe that the greatest blessing the Creator ever bestowed on me was when he permitted my external vision to be closed. He consecrated me for the work for which he created me…The loss of sight has been no loss for me…If I could meet (that doctor), I would tell him that he unwittingly did me the greatest favor in the world."

As we can see, God's technique for brokenness is a life-long process that begins with a shattering bedrock experience: an experience in which God strips us of every human prop and security; an experience through which God delivers the blow that initially crushes the hard outer shell of self-life; an experience that allows the Holy Spirit to begin to flow through us in genuine power.

GOD'S TARGET

In general, we may say that God's target in brokenness is our self-life. However, when it comes to God's bedrock shattering blow, we may identify a more specific target. Generally, God targets a person's greatest human strength — the source of their greatest security and confidence. Why? Because God is aiming to bring down the entire self-life system in that particular individual. To do so, he goes right to the heart of the matter.

God hits the flesh where it feels the strongest,

knowing that if he can bring a man or woman down at this point, the rest of their self-life will crumble as well. Therefore, it can be said that in the bedrock experience of brokenness, God goes for the jugular of the flesh.

If we look back at the scriptural examples we've examined, we can clearly see this principle in action.

- *Moses*

  What was Moses's greatest human strength? What was the thing that he prided himself on the most? It was his leadership, his generalship. Above all, Moses was sure of his ability to lead the Israelites. This was exactly where God let Moses fail in Exodus 2.

- *Peter*

  Peter's confidence rested in his courage, loyalty, bravery and valor. "Even if all fall away on account of you, I never will...Even if I have to die with you, I will never disown you" (Matt.26:33,35). And this was exactly where God let the blow fall in Peter's life.

- *Jacob*

  All Jacob's confidence was rooted in his self-resourcefulness, so God brought him low at that point. God put him in a situation in which all his cunning was worthless when he had to face Esau and his four-hundred armed men.

• *Isaiah*
  For Isaiah, it was self-righteousness. So God showed Isaiah the holiness of God and Isaiah was immediately gripped by a sense of his own vileness and corruption. God stripped Isaiah bare of his own righteousness. With the words "Woe to me! I am ruined" (Isa. 6:5), Isaiah confesses that his personal holiness has totally failed.

• *Abraham*
  For Abraham, it was his cherished son — that long-awaited son who God ordered Abraham to kill. As Abraham prepared to take the child's life, the Angel of the Lord called out "Do not lay a hand on the boy...now I know that you fear God because you have not withheld from me your son, your only son" (Gen. 22:12).

• *David*
  David's confidence was centered around his popularity and role as Israel's hero after killing Goliath. So God allowed him to be a fugitive and an outlaw — out of sight and out of mind in Israel for seven years.

- *Paul*

 Paul's confidence lay in his great Jewish pedigree (Phil. 3:4-6). He was a Pharisee; he had sat at the feet of the esteemed Rabbi Gamaliel (Acts 22:3); he had been rising in the ranks of Judaism faster than all his contemporaries. So God humbled Paul, stripping him of all position and sending him into the Arabian desert as a nobody for three years.

- *Joseph*

 Joseph's confidence lay in his status as dad's favorite and his dreams that promised him exaltation above all his brothers. And so God made him low man on the totem pole in prison in Egypt for thirteen years.

- *Job*

 Job's confidence was in his arrogant self-righteousness, which all his human prosperity fed and nurtured. And this is where God delivered the blow.

These examples confirm that God targets his shattering blow on those places that that the flesh declares strong.

IS GOD CRUEL?

You may be wondering why God works this way. You

may think it sounds brutal, even cruel. But this is only because we miss the point of what God is out to accomplish through brokenness. God is not just out to get our attention. Were that all God intended, he could accomplish it by less brutal means. Instead, God is out to shatter our self-resources. And he knows that the most effective way to do so is to strike at the point where our flesh feels the strongest and most secure. God knows that if he breaks our self-life at that point, all the other areas of self will come crashing down. It's inevitable.

I must add that God is not trying to radically change our personality or temperament. A weakness in a follower of Christ's life is nothing but a strength that is being misused.

Consider the biblical heroes we've discussed. God gave each of them their strong character qualities. The problem was that they were misusing their strengths. They were using them for the glory of self rather than the glory of God. They were using them in the energy of the flesh rather than in the power of the Spirit of God. So God wanted to transform the way they were using these qualities — from flesh-driven to Spirit-driven.

If we observe carefully, we find that the very areas where God struck the bedrock blow in these people's lives, became the areas of their greatest strength after brokenness. The difference is that these areas were now under the control of the Spirit and consecrated to the glory of God.

God's target in brokenness is a Christ-follower's human strengths. And God's goal is not to destroy these qualities but to purify them.

GOD'S TOOLS

The exact instrument that God chooses to accomplish the bedrock blow varies for every follower of Christ. Just as no doctor can use the same prescription for every patient, God cannot use the same hammer and anvil for every bedrock experience. Much depends upon the target. Certain weapons work better against certain targets. What I'm really saying is that God's brokenness strategy is unique for every believer in Jesus Christ.

Regardless of the specific tool he may choose, God's bedrock experience always involves failure, frustration, loss, setbacks, weakness, illness, heartache, suffering, disappointment, and pain. God never breaks anybody with success! God never delivers the crushing blow of brokenness by means of Bible study, prayer, sermons, witnessing, and fellowship.

Every Christ-follower that God has ever broken, he broke with human failure and loss. Listen to David's testimonial about his brokenness experience: "Before I was afflicted I went astray, but now I obey your Word" (Ps.119:67). And, "It was good for me to be afflicted so that I might learn your decrees" (Ps. 119:71).

The bottom line is that God uses affliction to break people. Even a casual look at brokenness reveals that affliction runs through its center like a mighty torrent. But this is not a bad thing. All of these peoples' failures, disappointments, and losses had a glorious purpose. They were all aimed at making these people throw themselves upon God. They were all aimed at destroying every source of human-based security in their lives. They were all aimed at driving them to total dependence upon God plus nothing.

These lessons can never be learned from success or prosperity. As Charles Stanley has aptly said: "Jesus is all we need — but we never learn that Jesus is all we need until Jesus is all we've got." This is why brokenness and failure come hand in hand. God must reduce us to the place where Jesus is all we've got.

Once again, when we walk through history and look at some of God's giants, this is exactly the way we find it to be. Failure and loss come before triumph.

Martin Luther

God broke this man with a year of hiding in the Castle of Wartburg. He was rejected by most of Europe and had a potential death sentence on his head should he have appeared in the open. Yet there in that cold, damp, deserted castle God converted a theology professor into a man of God. We picture Luther as a mighty crusader for biblical truth, but before he became that crusader, God let him experience deep failure and loss.

John Wesley

God broke this man with his abysmal failure as a missionary to the American Indians in Georgia. When he left Georgia in 1735, he had even managed to anger and alienate most of the settlers there. Wesley returned to England thoroughly discouraged. It was in this frame of mind that he entered Aldersgate Chapel in 1738 and felt his heart "strangely warmed," according to *The Journal of John Wesley*. There is some disagreement as to whether the Aldersgate experience represents Wesley's conversion or his full surrender. Either way, it is from this point that the power in Wesley's ministry began. And it grew out of failure and discouragement.

J. Hudson Taylor

God broke this great missionary to China through illness. After serving in China for six years, Taylor became so ill that he had to return to England. He became a virtual invalid and, at the age of twenty-nine doctors told him that he would never return to China. For five long, hidden years, Taylor was set aside — "shut up to prayer and patience" as he called it in his book, *Spiritual Secret*. Yet it was on this lonely sick bed that God developed Taylor into a man who could return to China and shake it with the gospel of Jesus Christ.

Adoniram Judson

God broke this great missionary to Burma through

tragedy and suffering. Judson buried his first wife and all of their children by her in Burma. Later, he buried a second wife in Burma. During most of his early years in Burma, Judson was in jail. There he did most of the work on the Burmese translation of the Bible. Judson ministered for six years before seeing his first convert. Yet out of all this hardship and heartache, God produced a man of great power. By the time of his death, Judson had seen sixty-three churches established with over seven thousand converts.

Robert E. Lee

Lee committed his life to Christ in the summer of 1853. He had had a brilliant military career in the U.S. Army before his conversion and was serving as superintendent of West Point. Many people only know of Lee as the celebrated general of the Army of Northern Virginia, which he commanded from June 1, 1862, until the end of the Civil War. However, Lee's first Confederate command was a complete failure. Lee was sent to defend Western Virginia (present-day West Virginia) and drive out the Federal troops in 1861. In reality, the Federals drove Lee out and Western Virginia was lost to the Confederacy forever.

Afterward, the press crucified Lee and the public sneered at him. They accused him of having an inflated reputation and nicknamed him Granny Lee, saying that he fought more like a grandmother than a soldier.

His next command was that of building earthworks and coastal defenses in South Carolina, not exactly what one would call strategic command. And there were many folks who complained that Lee wasn't even worthy of that assignment. We picture Lee as a gallant, invincible figure, mounted on Traveler. Indeed, God did use Lee in this way. But before that, God broke him with failure in the most coveted area of his life — his military ability.

Abraham Lincoln

God broke Lincoln with years of failure and hardship. At seven, he had to work to help support his family. At nine, his mother died. At twenty-three, a bad business deal left him with a debt that took him years to repay. At twenty-eight, he was snubbed by the girl he loved. At thirty-seven, he was finally elected to Congress on his third try. At thirty-nine, he failed to be reelected. About this time he had what we would call today a nervous breakdown. At forty-one, his four year old son died. At forty-three, he was defeated for land officer in Illinois. At forty-five, he ran for the U.S. Senate and lost. At forty-seven, his vice-presidential bid was rejected. At forty-nine, he ran for Senate and was defeated again. At fifty-one, he was elected president of the United States.

Fanny Crosby

Fanny Crosby was a perfectly normal little girl at her birth. When she was six months old, she developed an eye infection. Since the regular doctor was out of town, Crosby's parents had her treated by a physician in town who turned out to be incompetent. He put hot compresses on her eyes, scarring Crosby's corneas for life. Even the best surgeons in New York were unable to rectify the damage this quack doctor had done. Her parents were devastated. Yet, Crosby went on to become the most prolific American hymn writer in history. In her later years, she often said that she could never have written hymns as she did if she had been able to see. And she said if given the choice, she would choose for God to make her blind all over again.

A DARING PRAYER

At one time or another, as followers of Christ, so many of us have asked God to make us usable; to make us powerful servants of Jesus Christ; to do whatever is necessary to bring this to pass in our lives. When we pray such prayers, we are really asking God for brokenness. So God sends problems, suffering, and heartache our way. He sends failures, setbacks, and losses that are uniquely fitted for us. We so often refer to these things as tragedies.

But here's the real tragedy: our ignorance of the principles and process of brokenness often causes us to curse

God when all he's trying to do is answer our prayer. We often resist the process and resent the Lord for putting us through it simply because we don't understand how it all fits together in God's strategy for making us spiritually useable.

Nothing is accidental in a Christ-follower's life. God actively orders every detail. He knows those things that will most effectively shatter our self-life, and those are the things that he allows to come upon us. And whatever a loving God chooses for us — even though we would never have chosen it for ourselves — is best for us.

The process of brokenness may be distasteful, even devastating, but the product is worth it As noted author and speaker Chuck Swindoll said in *Growing Strong in the Seasons of Life*:

> What a strange lot we are! Enamored of the dazzling lights, and the splash of success, we seldom trace the lines that led to that flimsy and fleeting pinnacle. Bitter hardship. Unfair and undeserved abuses. Loneliness and loss. Humiliating failures. Debilitating disappointments...We resent those intruders. We treat them as enemies, not friends. We forget that...those who are really worth following have...come through the furnace melted, beaten, reshaped, and tempered.

Or to put it another way — they have been broken!

GOD'S ANSWER TO MY PRAYER

By 1991, things were looking good for me. I had been the senior pastor at McLean Bible for ten years. The church had successfully repositioned itself so that we could make an impact on the world around us. As a result of a churchwide vote of confidence, I had been granted a new mandate to lead.

The church was growing, averaging over one thousand people in attendance every weekend. It was poised to explode and become a significant launching pad for God in the D.C. area. It seemed like God was finally about to answer my prayer to be used in a mighty way for his kingdom and his glory.

But it was not to be. God knew I had become arrogant and wanted to grow the church for the wrong reasons. So he decided to throw me a curve ball and knock me back a few steps to reality. The timing of Jill's birth and subsequent illness was not an accident. God knew that before he could trust me with the kind of growth and influence he was going to send to McLean Bible he had to shatter me. Otherwise, the success was bound to go to my head, which would have ruined me and disgraced God's name.

Yes, the Lord was answering my prayer for maximum usefulness, but it would take me years to understand this. I was devastated, and I searched for a logical explanation for God's actions. Why was God doing this to me and my family? I came up with none. I searched my life for defiantly sinful behavior deserving of the Lord's discipline, but I found none.

I made matters worse by trying to control everything that was going wrong. I kept trying to fix Jill and her condition in my own human energy and wisdom. I demanded that God do a miracle and heal my daughter. No matter how hard I prayed, nothing seemed to change. No matter how I cried out to God, it felt like the heavens were made of brass. My prayers seemed to keep bouncing back at me, unheard and unanswered.

I finally reached the place where I had to release Jill and her health into the hands of God – to surrender her and turn it loose. I felt a lot like Abraham in Genesis 22, when God asked Abraham to sacrifice his son on an altar. Finally, I was done. The doctors told us Jill was going to die in 2000, and I was resigned to whatever God wanted.

Then, Jill began to improve – dramatically. She still couldn't speak, but she became engaged and responsive and regained her mobility. We could tell she was happy. Slowly, very slowly, Brenda and I felt hope seeping back into our lives. The dark cloud that had shrouded our emotions for nearly a decade began to lift.

When we emerged from the back side of the desert, we were two different people. This was especially true of me. People began telling me that my preaching had changed for the better, that it was becoming more tender, more sensitive, more real, more Spirit-empowered.

People said I was connecting with my congregation in a way I had never connected before. Many said that it was obvious that I had a whole new sensitivity to people and their hurts.

People began flocking to our church. Though we had no growth program (I had ceased to define my success by this measurement), people came by the thousands. The growth has continued to this day. We're now exceeding ten thousand each weekend.

Here's the point: God had done a work of brokenness in my life. He had knocked every human prop out from under me. He had smashed my self-sufficiency, my self-wisdom, and my self-resourcefulness. He had reduced me to *Jesus plus nothing*.

How did God do this? It's very simple. My greatest fear, indeed it was nearly a phobia, had always been that I would have a child with disabilities. I lived in mortal terror for nine months every time my wife was pregnant. When it came to my children's health, I was obsessed with fixing every minor and major problem. When any of the children were sick or injured, I walked around borderline depressed. I took them to the doctor at the slightest hint of a problem. I was engaged, resourceful, and, frankly, ultra-hyper. I considered it one of my greatest areas of strength. This is precisely where the Lord knew to hit me. And it worked.

Like Moody, in spite of all the pain, I wouldn't go back for anything.

DISCUSSION QUESTIONS

1. Do you agree that most people in life want the product without the process? How about you?

2. Do you feel that you have had the kind of bedrock, shattering experience that brought you to the end of yourself and your resources? Talk about it and how it altered your walk with God.

3. If God were to zero in on your greatest human strength for a brokenness experience, what would that strength be?

4. Where is God trying to break you? In what way are you resisting or resenting the process? In light of this chapter, how are you going to change your response to God? Why?

Nothing before, nothing behind
The steps of faith
Fall on the seeming void, and find
The rock beneath

~Hudson Taylor's *Spiritual Secret*~

CHAPTER FIVE

OPENING A HOLE IN THE DEFENSIVE LINE

Only as followers of Christ across America are broken, will we be in a position where revival fire can sweep over our land and overflow to touch the world. These days, a man may not attract great crowds preaching this kind of truth. But these are the issues that we must come to grips with if we are ever to see the power of God once again break out and overwhelm America.

Jehoshaphat, the king of Judah, summed up the attitude that lies at the heart of brokenness. When surrounded by a hostile army against which the army of Judah had no hope, he said: "O our God...for we have no power to face this vast army that is attacking us. We do not know what to do, but our eyes are upon you" (2 Chron. 20:12).

This is brokenness. No self-wisdom, no self-reliance, no self-sufficiency. This is total dependence upon God plus nothing: "our eyes are upon you"

The product is worth it. Like Enoch, broken Christians walk with God. Like Moses, broken Christians know the ways of God. Like Abraham, broken Christians are the friends of God. Like David, broken Christians are the apple of God's eye. Like Mary, broken Christians are highly favored and blessed. Broken Christians know a special intimacy and power with God.

All that we have said about brokenness so far leads to a logical question: if brokenness is so important, then why aren't more Christ-followers broken? The answer is that some things hinder God from breaking us. In this chapter, we will examine the four major hindrances to God's breaking process and learn how we can cooperate with God to see them breached.

THE HINDRANCE OF CONFUSION

This may well be the foremost obstacle to brokenness in an individual Christ-follower's life. So often, we're simply not sure what's going on when God begins to break us. As a result, we end up resisting and opposing God's attempts to do so, more out of confusion than anything else.

Very often, the basic introduction to the Christian life that we were given as young believers lies at the root of this confusion. Many of use were told to read our Bible, pray, witness, and fellowship and God will make our life smooth sailing. So we do all that we've been told to do and, instead, our life starts to fall apart. We go to our knees and begin searching for sin in our lives, but we find no areas of open, defiant disobedience to God. We search harder and still nothing shows up.

At this point we often become the victims of our ignorance about brokenness and trouble sets in. Rather than submitting to the process, we head off in other directions that work against what God is trying to do in breaking us. These other directions generally fall into one of two broad categories: anger and false guilt.

Anger

Sometimes, we get angry and begin to resist and resent the hand of God. Instead of submitting to God's attempts to break us, we try to weasel out of it anyway we can. We don't understand what's happening to us. We don't like it. We have trouble believing that it is truly from God. So at all cost we seek to avoid and escape it. When we can't, we become bitter toward God and our joy as Christ-followers dries up.

Depression and False Guilt

Other times we begin to cycle downward into false guilt and depression. We hear preachers telling us that Christ-followers who are walking with God and believing God will always be healthy, wealthy, prosperous, successful, and happy. Since we're not experiencing these things, we conclude that something is drastically wrong with us. Maybe God's angry with us for something. Maybe we're not really believing God like we should. Maybe we don't have the kind of faith that we need. Maybe this whole Christianity thing is a farce. Suddenly, false guilt, doubt, discouragement, despair, and even depression set in.

Job was a victim of this kind of confusion. God decided to do a work of bedrock brokenness in Job's life by stripping him of all his earthly possessions and even his health. But Job was ignorant of God's principles of brokenness. This ignorance about brokenness is what led to all of Job's angry outbursts, discouragement, and resistance to the hand of God. The whole book of Job is the record of Job's struggle to get a grip on what God was doing to him.

At the end of the book, when Job finally understood, he repented of his wrong attitudes and words. He said to God: "Surely I spoke of things I did not understand... Therefore I despise myself and repent in dust and ashes" (Job 42:3b,6).

Many of us as Christ-followers have been down the same route as Job. We have fought and resisted God's brokenness process simply because we did not understand it.

The solution to this hindrance lies with the preachers and Christian leaders of our day. We need to be taught biblically. We must be taught that God is out to break every one of us. We must be taught to recognize whose hand it is that is dealing with us. We must be taught that all pain and sickness and failure and loss are not from the devil. We must be taught that God himself sends these experiences into our lives, just like God sent them into Job's life, to accomplish his divine purposes.

We must be taught that the brokenness experiences that God sends our way are for our highest good, that trying to escape them is foolishness, and that brokenness experiences are part of God preparing us for the best he has for us! A well-taught Christ-follower never tries to escape the cross in his or her life. But, many sincere, yet confused Christ-followers have delayed God's brokenness in their lives for years by resisting and evading God's every attempt to break them.

When trials and struggles come into our lives we must begin by examining our life for deliberate sin. But if we find none, we should simply assume that God is trying to break us a little more or for the first time, as the case may be. Some of us need to pray a prayer like this one:

"Lord, you've been working on me for all these years. But I have been so foolish. I didn't understand. I resisted your hand. I've tried to escape everything you've sent to break me. But now I see your hand, Lord. I see your blessed purpose and I'm willing to surrender myself to you fully today. Oh God, do your work in me."

THE HINDRANCE OF SELF-DECEPTION

As Watchman Nee points out so well, if God is to break us, he must get us to see ourselves as we really are. He must get us to see ourselves as he sees us. He must get us to acknowledge the self-sins that are hindering the power of God in our lives. The difficulty is that we are masters at deceiving ourselves about ourselves. So, as a prerequisite to breaking us, God must strip away our false notions of what we are.

This is exactly what happens in John, chapter 21, when Jesus confronts Peter over the issue of Peter's love for Him. In verse 15, Jesus asks Peter whether he has *agape* for him — that is, self-sacrificial love for him. Peter could not bring himself to say that he does, because he had just denied Jesus three times. So Peter declares that he has *philos* for Jesus that is, warm human affection.

Peter must have thought that this admission of lesser love for Jesus would have satisfied the Lord's probing question. But it didn't. And the reason was that Peter was still kidding himself about himself.

In verse 17, Jesus questions Peter further, asking him if he even has *philos* for him. The Bible says that Peter was sad because he sensed that Jesus was challenging him even on his watered-down confession of his feelings for Jesus. So Peter was forced to say, "Lord, you know all things..."

Do you see what Jesus is doing with Peter? God orchestrated the events of Peter's denial to bring a bedrock brokenness experience to bear on Peter's life. And yet, even after that humiliating failure, Peter still had not quite come to the point where God wanted him. He was still deceiving himself about himself. You see, the truth was that Peter, at this point in his life, really had both *agape* and *philos* for only one person — himself!

This is how Jesus saw Peter's heart. Jesus was not angry with Peter. He was simply trying to get Peter to see the true state of his heart and admit it to himself. Jesus was out to get Peter to stop deceiving himself about himself, because God could not break him or change him until he did.

We too must let God show us our hearts as he sees them. When that happens, we make some startling discoveries. Whereas once we said that we loved the Lord, under God's searchlight we find that we really love ourselves. Whereas we once said that we were zealous for the Lord, under God's searchlight we find that our zeal is really driven by human energy and desire for recognition. Whereas once we said that we were serving the Lord for his glory, under God's searchlight we find that our service comes more from our love of action, our delight in speaking, and our desire to earn a reputation among the saints.

The deeper we allow God's searchlight to shine in our hearts, the more unbroken self we begin to see there. So much of what we once called God's work turns out to be just carnal activity. We begin to see in our conversations, activities, works, zeal, witnessing, and acts of service how all-pervading our self-life really is. God brings us low before him as we begin to realize this.

This sounds like a negative and destructive process, but it is exactly the opposite. Despite the pain of such self-discovery, God seasons the whole process with his tender love and comfort so that we can rejoice through the tears. The result is a glorious one: we start to long for and beg God to break the grip that self has on every part of our life.

The solution to this second hindrance to brokenness is for us to have courage to ask God to show us ourselves as we really are. We must learn to pray as David did: "Test me, O Lord, and try me. Examine my heart and my mind" (Ps. 26:2). "Search me, O God, and know my heart; test me and know my anxious thoughts. See if there is any offensive way in me..." (Ps. 139:23-24).

When God is pleased to answer our prayer, we must respond with the courage to face the truth squarely, without justification or rationalizations. Broken Christians are people who are willing to get real and honest with God and with themselves.

THE HINDRANCE OF FEAR

Brokenness terrifies us. We're scared of what brokenness

is going to require of us. We're scared of what God may do to us. We're scared of the cost of being broken. Parents fear that it will cost them their child. Business people fear that it will cost them their careers. Some fear that it will cost them their health and wealth.

The result of this fear is spiritual paralysis. Such fear causes us to take our eyes off Jesus and put them on the circumstances that we're so afraid may come our way. It causes us to forget about the grace, mercy, strength, and joy that God promises to give us in our brokenness experiences. Therefore, fear causes us to shrink back from surrendering to God's will in breaking us.

The solution to this hindrance is for us to cling to God's promises. Biblical truth is the only effective antidote for fear. The Bible tells us that God's perfect love casts out fear (1 John 4:18). In other words, resting in God's deep love and concern for us will cast out our fear.

We must remember that God will never ask anything of us unless he is prepared to walk with us hand in hand. He will sustain us every step of the way. As has been said, the will of God will never lead us where the grace of God will not keep us.

But we never get grace until we need it. We get dying grace when we're ready to die; bad-neighbor grace when we have a bad neighbor; single-parent grace when we become one; getting-fired grace when we lose our jobs.

By the same token, we get brokenness grace when we need it. For us to focus on hypothetical crises that God might use to break us, without taking into account the grace of God that will be there when we need it, is to condemn ourselves to spiritual bondage and paralysis.

In 1983, my two-year-old son fell out of the car while we were coming off an entrance ramp curve and accelerating to get on the interstate. It was late at night and, in an instant, he accidentally opened the door and was sucked out of the car.

As I ran back toward his limp little body, lying face-down in the road, watching as cars swerved to dodge him, the grace of God was so overwhelming, so irresistible, so overpowering that it is downright indescribable. I had never experienced anything like it before in my life. As we raced to the emergency room, there was no panic or protest in my heart, just the calm of the Spirit of God. I am happy to report that God saw fit to spare my little boy's life. But in those awful moments, God taught me a great lesson.

You see, if someone had told me in advance that this was going to happen, I would have fretted and feared and been spiritually immobilized. I would have been focusing on a future trial — but without the future grace.

As we approach brokenness, we must focus on Jesus. We must remind ourselves of his absolute promise of grace to face every trial. We must remind ourselves of the compassion, comfort, and strength that he provides with every trial. We must be confident of His love and mercy. The solution to our fear is to keep our eyes fixed on Jesus.

THE HINDRANCE OF STUBBORNNESS

Whenever God begins to break us, our stubborn human pride always becomes an issue. We have to confront this question: am I willing to let God do what he wants to do in my life, even though I may not like it or fully understand it?

At this point, we are beyond confusion, for we know what brokenness is about now. We are beyond self-deception, for we know what we are about now. We are beyond fear, for we know what Jesus has promised us.

Now we are at the point of surrender: either we will submit to God or we won't; either we will let God break us or we won't. We often cover this up cosmetically with a lot of rationalizations and excuses. But the bottom line is whether we are going to submit to God's way or insist on our own. "For the outward man to be broken, a full consecration is imperative," Nee wrote in *The Release of the Spirit*. "Consecration is merely an expression of our willingness to be in the hands of God."

It is tragic how many Christ-followers are sitting in churches across the world with their stubborn will set to resisting God. In spite of God's efforts to break them, they have determined that they will not be humbled or have their pride shattered. As a result, they have seen their spiritual lives shrivel up. The joy, the power, and the anointing of God are gone. In their place are spiritual stagnation and coldness of heart.

This is tragic, and it is the result of stubborn, fleshly pride. When we examine the Bible, we can find numerous stubborn people like this. The rich young ruler described in Matthew 19 is one such example. Jesus requested that this man give all his belongings to the poor and then come follow him.

Many readers misunderstand this passage. They assume that Jesus was requiring the man to make this kind of sacrifice in order to have eternal life. That is not the case. What Jesus wants to produce by this demand is not salvation but brokenness. This man's confidence and security was in his riches. Jesus was calling on him to let it all go and rely on Jesus alone.

This would have been this man's shattering blow of brokenness. Out of the ashes, Jesus would have produced an abundant life unlike anything this young man could imagine.

He was perched at the crossroads. But his stubborn will and his pride refused to yield to God. Tragically, the Bible declares that "he went away sorrowful" (Matt. 19:22), and he was never to be heard of again in the annals of the kingdom of God.

The solution to the hindrance of stubbornness is simply to surrender and let God have his way. Until we do, we're at a stalemate. God can't go any further in our lives until we surrender and let him break us where he wants to.

FROM PREACHING TO MEDDLING

Here I'm going from preaching to meddling.

Where is it that God is trying to break you? Where have you been unwilling to let him? Has God delivered a crushing blow to you? Are you still angry with him — and at war with him in your heart? What has God been asking you to do but your stubborn pride has refused because it would have brought you low? Where has your stubborn human will set itself in determined opposition to the breaking process of God in your life?

We either say yes or no to God. When it comes to brokenness, there is no straddling the fence. We must either surrender to God and let him have his way, or we will resist God and hinder the process of brokenness in our lives. Brokenness demands total surrender and there is simply no other way.

One of the saddest spectacles in God's kingdom is a Christ-follower who has fought God, resisted God, and wasted years on the backside of the desert. Such Christ followers never achieve the brokenness that leads to true spiritual power and usefulness. All these believers have to look back on is the haunting thought of what they could have been and done, if they had only let God have his way in their lives.

Brokenness before God is the sweetest experience

that a human being can have. But you and I can only get there by making the deliberate choices that allow God to accomplish this result in our lives.

MY ENCOUNTER WITH THE HINDRANCES

When the Lord sent Jill into my life, I had a pastor's basic knowledge of brokenness but didn't fully understand how deeply I needed it. I was blind to the fact that I was caught in the grip of all four hindrances: confusion, self-deception, fear, and stubbornness. Rather than embrace brokenness, I ran away from it – as fast as I could.

I was confused by what the Lord was doing to me and, as a result, became angry and depressed. I was deeply deceived about the true status of my heart before God. My genuine desire to use McLean Bible Church to honor God was clouded by personal ambition and ego. I scoffed when others warned me of this. God knew what had to be done, that he needed to take me on a journey of honest self-discovery. But I was fearful of how he would do it, scared of the pain and suffering that God has used on his other servants. I was trying hard to make it to the end of my life without enduring such rigors.

Until 1992, I did a good job of avoiding the obvious. I knew very little about the all-sufficient grace of God that Paul boasted of in 2 Corinthians 12:9: "But he said to me, 'My grace is sufficient for you, for my power is made perfect in weakness.'" I knew plenty of Bible verses and promises in my head, but I had never been forced to depend on God plus nothing of myself as deeply as I had to as Jill became progressively sicker.

Much of my resistance came from being stubborn. Frankly, I had a surrender problem. I wanted to serve the Lord, but I wanted to do it on my own terms. I wanted to dictate the conditions and map out a plan. I was willing to accept minor course corrections, but not radical departures. I felt I knew what the Lord had called me to do and I was busy getting it done, on my terms. I was like Moses in Exodus 2, so God needed to bring me to a place of absolute surrender to his plan, done his way, by his methods, in his time.

So here I was with all four hindrances – the defensive linemen of the flesh – standing opposite me. To advance the ball for Christ, a hole needed to be opened in that defensive line. God used Jill to do it. I didn't have to do anything (in the energy of the flesh) to deal with my confusion, self-deception, fear, and stubbornness. The Lord did it. My part was simply to come to my senses and trust his hand and believe his heart. Sometimes it was really hard to do, but the alternative – to distrust the Lord and doubt his leading in my life – was unacceptable to me.

The result is that I discovered that God makes no mistakes and he wastes no experiences. I learned that he loves me as deeply as he says and that the painful experiences he sent me flow from his unconditional dedication to make me a better, healthier, and more spiritually useable person for the sake of his glory. If you're a Christ-follower and you're going through deep waters, please be assured that the Lord feels exactly this same way about you. But if the four hindrances exist in your life as they did in mine, God needs to expose and excise them in order to make your life really count for him.

As you go through the process of brokenness, you must never lose sight of biblical truth and never mistrust God's hand or doubt his heart. In the midst of a very trying time, David wrote these words in Psalm 77:1, 2, 7-9:

> I cried out to God for help;
> I cried out to God to hear me.
> When I was in distress, I sought the Lord;
> at night I stretched out untiring hands
> and my soul refused to be comforted.
> Will the Lord reject forever?
> Will he never show his favor again?
> Has his unfailing love vanished forever?
> Has his promise failed for all time?
> Has God forgotten to be merciful?
> Has he in anger withheld his compassion?

These sound like the questions I began to ask God in

1992. You've probably asked these same questions yourself. So what's the answer? David goes on to tell us:

> Your ways, O God, are holy...
> With your mighty arm you redeemed your
>   people...
> Your path led through the sea,
> your way through the mighty waters,
> though your footprints were not seen.
> You led your people like a flock...
> (*Ps. 77:13-20, excerpted*)

In the wilderness after the exodus, God was leading his people Israel like a flock even when they couldn't see or understand how God was doing so. David's point is clear: even when I can't trace God's footprints, I can still trust God's heart. God's hand is always trustworthy, his heart is always true, and his presence is always there, even in the darkest of circumstances.

DISCUSSION QUESTIONS

1. Have you ever been angry with God for trouble he's sent into your life?
2. How have you resisted God's attempts to break you in the past? Are you still doing this today or have you truly given God your full surrender?

3. Have you ever allowed God to turn the searchlight on your heart and its self-sins? Talk about this experience and what you discovered about yourself.

4. Can you relate to the idea that fear about brokenness might produce spiritual paralysis in your walk with God?

5. Are you and God at a stalemate? Are you willing to surrender to God and let him have 100 percent authority in your life?

*Spiritual leaders are not made by theological training
or ministry appointment. Only God Himself
can produce a truly anointed man or woman of God.
Religious position can be conferred by bishops and
synods, but not spiritual authority.
Spiritual authority is a thing of the Spirit.*

~J. Oswald Sanders, *Spiritual Leadership*~

CHAPTER SIX

THE PRODUCT IS WORTH THE PROCESS

There is nothing so beautiful in God's sight, or powerful in God's hand, as a Christ-follower who has been broken. As we have seen, brokenness is a bloody process. Thus far we have focused much attention on how painful the process can be. In this chapter, I want to focus on the products of brokenness, because we have been holding on to the promise that the product is worth the process.

The products of brokenness are most dramatically seen and experienced in three areas of life: our relationship with God, our relationship with people, and our service for Jesus Christ. Let's examine each in turn.

OUR RELATIONSHIP WITH GOD

One of the greatest products of brokenness is a new

intimacy with Almighty God. Broken followers of Christ know God in a way that other people — even other followers of Christ — do not. Broken followers of Christ have an intimacy with God that they never had before. The reason for this is rooted in the very nature and character of God:

"For this is what the high and lofty One says — he who lives forever, whose name is holy: 'I live in a high and holy place, but also with him who is contrite and lowly in spirit, to revive the spirit of the lowly and to revive the heart of the contrite'" (*Isa. 57:15*).

"This is what the Lord says, 'Heaven is my throne, and the earth is my footstool. Where is the house you will build for me? Where will my resting place be?...This is the one I esteem: he who is humble and contrite in spirit, and trembles at my word'" (*Isa. 66:1,2b*).

"The sacrifices of God are a broken spirit; a broken and contrite heart, O God, you will not despise" (*Ps. 51:17*).

"The Lord is close to the brokenhearted and saves those who are crushed in spirit" (*Ps. 34:18*).

"He heals the brokenhearted and binds up their wounds....The Lord delights in those who fear him, who put their hope in his unfailing love" (*Ps. 147:3,11*)

The Bible tells us that broken followers of Christ become God's special friends. God takes special delight in them. God reveals more of himself to them, not because he loves them more than other Christ-followers, but because he is able to communicate himself to them in deeper, more intimate ways. This truth can be seen so clearly in the life of Moses. After God had broken him, Moses enjoyed a beautiful intimacy with God. This is stated clearly in Psalm 103:7: "He made known his ways to Moses, his deeds to the people of Israel." In other words, the children of Israel, who were definitely not a broken bunch, saw God's deeds. But Moses got to know God's ways.

The Bible also describes this great intimacy between God and Moses in Exodus 33:11a: "The Lord would speak to Moses face to face, as a man speaks with his friend." What an amazing depth of personal intimacy.

This experience is not unique to Moses, however. Every broken believer has known this type of intimacy with God.

- Abraham was the friend of God (2 Chron. 20:7).
- Jacob testified that he had seen God face to face (Gen. 32:30).

- David was the apple of God's eye (Ps. 17:8).
- D.L. Moody said in *The Life of Dwight L. Moody*, "I can only say that God revealed himself to me and I had such an experience of his love that I had to ask him to stay his hand."

Out of this deep and intimate walk with God, Abraham, Jacob, and David made their impact on the world. It was out of this intimacy with God that Moody preached with earthshaking power, as did Spurgeon, Finney, Wesley, and Whitefield.

Out of this intimacy with God, Fanny Crosby wrote more than eight-thousand hymns, George Muller shook the heavens in prayer, and Robert Murray McCheyne began the revival that shook all Scotland. And through such intimacy Hudson Taylor, Adoniram Judson, William Carey, David Brainerd, and Mother Theresa rocked the mission field with the message of Jesus Christ.

These men and women knew a special closeness with God that came from being broken. God was more real to them, God's heart was more exposed to them, and God's Word was more understandable to them than to the masses of churchgoers around them. God revealed his ways to them and shared the deeper parts of himself with them in a unique fashion.

As God begins to break us, one of the first results that we notice is a new sense of the closeness of God. It is not a theological closeness, nor a doctrinal closeness, but an experiential closeness — a tender intimacy with God that we have never experienced before.

One of the wonderful and practical outworkings of this intimacy with Christ is a new ability to rest calmly in Jesus regardless of the raging storms of life. Things that would have sent our anxiety level soaring — things that would have preoccupied us with worry and fretting — we are now able to give to Jesus and simply leave with him.

This explains why Hudson Taylor's favorite hymn was "Jesus, I am resting, resting, In the joy of what Thou art."

It explains how Fanny Crosby could write *Safe in the Arms of Jesus*:

> Free from the blight of sorrows, free from my
> doubts and fears
> Only a few more trials, only a few more tears
> Safe in the arms of Jesus, Safe on His gentle
> breast
> There by His love o'ershadowed, Sweetly my
> soul shall rest.

Broken Christ-followers know what it means to have the peace of God that passes all understanding — even in the middle of tumultuous circumstances. They know how to rest in the Lord and wait patiently for him. They understand that, sometimes, God's will for his followers is for them simply to stand still and know that he is God. Brokenness allows them to do it.

If God gave us nothing else out of brokenness except this deep and special intimacy with himself — this alone would make it all worth it.

OUR RELATIONSHIP WITH PEOPLE

Watchmen Nee and Charles Stanley are right when they say that brokenness also has a wonderful effect on our relationships with others. I have identified five characteristics in broken Christ-followers that influence their relationships with other people. Broken Christ-followers are approachable, teachable, sensitive, turfless, and forgiving. Let's examine these traits more closely.

Approachable

Broken Christ-followers are approachable people who are easy to talk to, easy to ask questions of, and easy to open up to. There is a softness about broken followers of Christ. They are comfortable and relaxing to be around. Every encounter with them leaves us feeling uplifted, encouraged, and spiritually strengthened.

Broken Christ-followers also find it easy to humble themselves before others. They can quickly admit when they are wrong and they are not defensive when they are criticized. If you tell such a person that you think they're wrong you won't find them bristling up like a porcupine. They don't respond with excuses and rationalizations. Instead, they display a genuine openness and willingness to listen.

It is astounding how many porcupine Christians are out there. They walk around with all their needles laid down — until you cross them! But when you try to make them do something they don't want to do, or you tell them they're incorrect about something, or cause them to lose face in some way, then suddenly all of the needles bristle to attention.

When God breaks us, he takes all the porcupine out of us. You see, broken Christ-followers no longer have any vain ego to defend. They have already lost all face before God, so to lose face before men is no big deal. They have been utterly humbled by God and they have nothing left to protect.

Moses demonstrated this approachable spirit when his father-in-law Jethro in Exodus 18 rebuked him. Now, Moses was the one who had brought the plagues upon Egypt, the one who had brought mighty Pharaoh to his knees, and the one who had opened the Red Sea. He could have easily responded to Jethro with an attitude like this: who do you think you are to correct me?

But Moses was a broken man. And, as a result, he was an approachable man. He listened without defensiveness to Jethro and took his good advice.

As God breaks us, we will find ourselves becoming

more approachable, less defensive, more humble, more able to admit that we're wrong, and more able to accept criticism without paranoia or excuses. Approachability is one of the beautiful and tender qualities that God gives to broken Christ-followers.

Teachable

A broken Christ-follower has learned that they do not know as much as they once thought they did. In fact, the more God breaks us, the more skeptical we become of our own human wisdom and judgment. We begin to develop an overwhelming need for God's wisdom, even if God chooses to send it to us through other people. We find ourselves more willing to listen to others. We become genuinely teachable.

Again, Moses illustrates this point. After Jethro rebuked Moses and offered him advice, Moses immediately recognized his father-in-law's wisdom. "So Moses listened to his father-in-law and did everything he said" (Exod. 18:24).

As the example of Moses shows us, one of the marks of true brokenness is that we begin to admit to ourselves that we aren't as wise as we thought we were. When a person gets to this point, God can finally begin to make them genuinely wise.

Sensitive

A broken Christian has an uncanny ability to sense

where other people are — spiritually, emotionally, and psychologically. Broken Christians are able to sense movement in other people's spirits, to sense non-verbal messages from them and to sense when others are hurt, disappointed, struggling, uncomfortable, scared, jealous, angry, frustrated or confused.

This sensitivity is not a conscious or contrived thing. It is a product of brokenness. As the Holy Spirit is released in our spirit he automatically gives us a deep sensitivity to the spirits of other people.

In Numbers 11, we see this sensitivity in Moses's life. Joshua told Moses that two everyday Israelites, Eldad and Medad, were prophesying back in the camp. Although Joshua never said to Moses exactly what was in his heart, Moses knew. Joshua pretended to be concerned for Moses's prestige and authority but Moses saw his true motivation. He said to Joshua: "Are you jealous for my sake? I wish that all the LORD'S people were prophets, and that the LORD would put His spirit on them!" (Num. 11:29)

Moses saw right through Joshua. Joshua's attempt to conceal his own jealously by claiming to be concerned for Moses may have fooled others but not Moses. Moses's spirit could sense with a supernatural discernment where Joshua's spirit really was. In response, Moses was able to deal with Joshua at his real point of need.

This is one reason why broken Christians make the

best counselors, confidants and friends. They are able to cut through the smoke and mirrors and get down to the real issues of a person's spirit.

Turfless

A broken Christian knows that all they are, all they have, and all they will ever be is due totally to the grace of God. They know that any position they may presently hold, any riches they may presently possess, any honor they may presently enjoy, or any power they may presently wield is all the result of the sovereign will of God.

They know that God is as free to take these things as he was to give them. What all this means is that a broken follower of Christ has no personal turf to protect.

As a result, when a broken Christ-follower's position or authority or reputation or power is threatened, they respond by simply resting in God. Their strategy is to allow God to defend their prerogatives if God wants these privileges to continue. Since these prerogatives are the gift of God, there's no need for the broken Christ-follower to fight for them. The same God who gave them can defend and preserve them by his own supernatural power.

The broken Christ-follower knows that God needs no help from us in this arena and that he prefers none. Therefore, the broken Christ-follower does not feel insecure in leaving their defense totally in the hands of his God.

Moses gives us a splendid illustration of this principle in action in Numbers 12. Here, Miriam and Aaron rise up and challenge Moses's authority. They summon all their courage, plan for Moses's every response, and prepare to take Moses on. "Miriam and Aaron began to talk against Moses because of his Cushite wife, for he had married a Cushite" (Num. 12:1).

Their strategy to unseat Moses was to criticize him for his marriage to a non-Hebrew woman. Their goal was to strip him of his power and authority and to replace him with themselves. "'Has the Lord spoken only through Moses?'" they asked. 'Hasn't he also spoken through us?'" (Num. 12:2).

It was a case of clear mutiny. How did Moses respond? Simply put, Moses did nothing! Verse 3 tells us why. "Now Moses was a very meek man, more meek than anyone else on the face of the earth."

Meekness is not weakness. It is a spiritual attitude that says: Lord, it's not my authority and power being threatened, it's yours. You gave it to me. If you want to take it away and give it to someone else, that's up to you. And if you want me to keep it for the time being, then you defend me, Lord!

Miriam and Aaron soon found out that they had taken on a whole lot more than Moses. By the time God had finished defending Moses, Miriam and Aaron were fortunate to have escaped with their lives (Num. 12:8-11).

Like Moses, broken Christ-followers are comfortable with leaving their defense to God. When we do this, we find — just as Moses did — that God always does a better job defending us than we do.

This attitude of turflessness,or spiritual meekness, leaves us free to interact with people in a relaxed and non-defensive posture. It liberates us. It revolutionizes our relationships.

Forgiving

Broken Christ-followers have learned to see God's hand in all that people do to them. They have a godly view of their circumstances. They understand the truth of Romans 8:28: "And we know that in all things, God works for the good of those who love him, who have been called according to his purpose." Broken people have seen this verse come true in their lives.

Broken followers of Christ can look back and see how God used even the unkind and hurtful things that people have done to them as part of his blessed breaking process. It's no longer a question what someone did to them. Instead, they see that the person was simply God's instrument and their mistreatment was all part of God's plan. They can see that mistreatment actually enabled God to work in their life.

When this transformation in outlook takes place —

and it always does when God breaks us — it totally changes our response to mistreatment. Holding grudges becomes unthinkable. Bitterness becomes unacceptable. And forgiveness comes easily and naturally because we see so clearly that people are merely tools in the hands of Almighty God.

Suddenly, we find ourselves able to respond to people who've hurt us as Joseph responded to his brothers who so vilely mistreated him. They sold him into slavery in Egypt and Joseph forgave them freely and completely. When they asked him why he was so willing to forgive them, Joseph gave them this answer. "And now, do not be distressed and do not be angry with yourselves for selling me here, because it was to save lives that God sent me ahead of you...so then it was not you who sent me here, but God." (Gen. 45:5,8). And further, "You intended to harm me, but God intended it for good..." (Gen 50:20a).

We also see this forgiveness illustrated in Moses's life. Remember how Miriam plotted against him, planned his overthrow, betraying her relationship with her little brother? This person, who watched over his deliverance from the Nile, planned to watch over his downfall.

As a result, God struck Miriam with leprosy — and a serious case at that. Moses's natural human response would have been to rejoice that now she has gotten hers! Retribution is sweet to the flesh.

But this was not the response of Moses at all. Moses forgave her, fully and freely and quickly. Moses felt immediate compassion for her and prayed fervently for her healing "So Moses cried out to the LORD, 'O God, please heal her!'" (Num. 12:13).

Like Moses and Joseph, broken Christ-followers discover a new freedom to forgive people from the heart. It's not something that they contrive by the energy of the flesh. It is a supernatural freedom, set loose by the Spirit of God. Forgiveness is one of the great legacies of brokenness. And it forever changes how a broken follower of Christ relates to the world.

As God begins to break us, we find that suddenly people are attracted to us. They begin opening up and sharing things because they feel safe with us. God's brokenness creates an atmosphere around us in which people feel relaxed, comfortable, and unthreatened. As you can see, brokenness is an essential commodity if we are to be used by God in the lives of others.

OUR SERVICE FOR GOD
Because brokenness affects our relationship with God and with others, it dramatically impacts our service for Christ. As I've said, the ultimate purpose of God in breaking us is so that he can use us. Brokenness brings new spiritual power into a person's life and new effectiveness in service to God. Every broken follower of

Christ testifies to this new influx of power, anointing, and fruitfulness. What is the source of this new power? It is the Holy Spirit, of course, who is now free to move without hindrance in a life whose outer shell of self has been shattered by God. Brokenness lowers our spiritual resistance, allowing the Spirit to flow freely out of our lives. This is the most exciting and dynamic part of brokenness: God uses it to make us a channel for the Holy Spirit's power.

Let's look at some examples of this truth. If you look at Moses's life during his first eighty years, you will find that very little of God's spiritual power flowed through him.

It is interesting that Moses appears in well over a hundred chapters of the Old Testament, but only two deal with the first eighty years of his life. At first glance, this might seem to be an imbalance. But the truth is, Moses did virtually nothing during these first eighty years of any lasting spiritual value, so why write about it! And the reason Moses accomplished so little of lasting spiritual value in those first eighty years is that he was unbroken.

But after Moses had been broken by God, he became an eternal example of the power of God pulsating through a man's life: the ten plagues, the opening of the Red Sea, the water from the rock, the manna, the quail, the Ten Commandments, and scores of other manifestations of God's power that came through him in the wilderness. The difference between the power of God operating through Moses's last forty years and in his first eighty years can be summed up in one word: brokenness.

In the same way, Isaiah wrote the greatest prophecy ever written — after he was broken. Paul became the greatest missionary that the world has ever known and wrote the bulk of the New Testament — after he was broken. Fanny Crosby became the most prolific American hymn writer in history — after she was broken. It was the same with Dwight L. Moody. After his experience with brokenness, according to his biography, *The Life of Dwight L. Moody*, Moody said, "The sermons were not different...I did not present any new truth. And yet now hundreds were converted."

Do we hear what Moody is saying; no new truths, no new messages, no new methods? But suddenly, the convicting power of the Holy Spirit began to flow through him as never before. Why? Because Moody was a broken vessel that God could fully use.

Moody went to England in 1873, not intending to hold any meetings there. Two years and one week later, Moody returned to America after being at the center of the greatest revival to sweep England since the days of Wesley over a century before.

At one particular service in England, the meeting hall was so full that Moody himself could not even get in to preach! And there were some twenty to thirty thousand more people standing outside the hall. Moody brought the whole crowd outdoors and preached to them by standing on the seat of an open buggy. The choir led the singing from the roof of a nearby shed. More than ten thousand people came forward to give their lives to Jesus Christ!

Moody's ministry career became one mighty event like this after another. God used Moody to preach to over 100 million people, and, as his biographer, W.R. Moody, said, "Moody was personally responsible for reducing the population of hell by one million souls."

It was the same with John Wesley. We have seen how God used his missionary failure in the Georgia colony to break him. After he returned to England and settled his relationship with Christ at Aldersgate Chapel, the power of God began to vibrate through his life. He began preaching in the open air and thousands were converted in meeting after meeting. The Spirit of God was so mighty in his meetings that Wesley wrote in *The Journal of John Wesley*, "My voice could scarcely be heard above the groaning of some and the cries of others, calling aloud to him that is mighty to save."

During his itinerant ministry of some fifty years, Wesley traveled over 225,000 miles on horseback and preached over forty thousand sermons of two to three hours in length. Through John Wesley, God literally turned eighteenth-century England upside-down for Jesus Christ.

Once Wesley said, "Give me one hundred preachers who fear nothing but sin and desire nothing but God — and I care not whether they be clergymen or laymen — such men alone will shake the gates of hell and set up the Kingdom of Heaven on earth."

The point is that Wesley understood the kind of people that God uses. He understood that God can do more through one broken Christ-follower than he can through fifty unbroken ones. That's why Wesley looked for broken people to assist him in the ministry.

Let's consider one more example — Charles G. Finney. Finney was born in Connecticut in 1792. He grew up to be a lawyer who was intensely cynical about Christianity and the reality of Jesus Christ. But in 1821, God not only brought him to faith in Christ but God totally broke him. Finney's problem was pride and God utterly shattered that pride bringing Finney down to the dust before him. Finney was soon preaching Christ and holding revival meetings throughout New England. Sometimes the power of God was so great in his meetings that entire audiences would fall on their knees in prayer and confession of sin.

Finney's revival meetings had such effects upon the communities where they were held that, often a decade later, their effects were still being felt. There are testimonials of God's power falling with such impact on cities where Finney was holding meetings that unbelievers came under the conviction of sin upon simply entering the city limits.

In his revival meetings of 1857-59, according to the book, *Deeper Experiences of Famous Christians*, some six hundred thousand souls were brought to Christ in what Dr. Lyman Beecher called "the greatest work of God and the greatest revival of religion that the world has ever seen." So great was Finney's power to burn the need for holy living into people's hearts, that of these six hundreds thousand folks, actual records show that some eighty five percent of them remained committed to Jesus Christ years later.

While he was in Utica, New York for a series of meetings, Finney visited a large factory, where he was recognized by one of the workers. At the mere sight of Finney, this worker came under the deep conviction of sin and sank to his knees, breaking down and weeping. Soon, another did the same, and another, until so many workers were sobbing and crying out to God because of their sin that the whole factory was shut down while Finney preached to them about the love and forgiveness of God!

This is what power from God is all about, and God only gives it to broken Christ-followers. God has not changed since Moses's day. He has not changed since Moody and Wesley and Finney's day. I am convinced that God still yearns to sweep through factories and cities and nations as he has done before. I am convinced that such movements of God are still possible in our day— despite all the forces of hell that are arrayed against them.

I am convinced that the power from God that these people knew can be had today. I am convinced that God is aching to see the Spirit of God move today like he did in these peoples ministries. But it cannot happen until there are Christ-followers who are willing to pay the price — and the price is brokenness.

Not every broken follower of Christ will be another Finney or Moody. Such ministries belong exclusively to the sovereign will and plan of God. But any Christ-follower who will allow God to break them will see a new intimacy with God, a new level of relationship with people, and a new power for service in their life. God will give those believers greater fruitfulness for Jesus than they've ever known or dreamed possible.

There is a great difference between Christian activity and true spiritual power — the kind of power that comes from God breaking a life. Maximum usefulness comes from maximum brokenness, and the more fully we allow God to break us, the more fully God can and will use us. No one ever experienced brokenness like the Apostle Paul, and no one ever affected the world for Jesus Christ like Paul did either. Brokenness and greatness for God always have and always will go hand in hand.

WAS BROKENNESS REALLY WORTH IT?

I've often wondered what decision I'd make if God were to take me back in time to before Jill was born, and offer me a choice: perfect health for my daughter or brokenness for me. In light of what the Lord has done in my life, in my family, and in my ministry through Jill's illness, I honestly know the right choice would be to say: Lord, you make no mistakes. Let it happen just like you chose the first time. The products were worth the process.

My flesh being what it is, however, I'm afraid that if the Lord were to give me the chance, I would make the wrong choice. I'd choose Jill's perfect health, even though it would mean that my service to the Lord would be a mere shadow of what it has become. Perhaps this is why the Lord will never offer me – or you – such a choice.

So, was the product really worth the process? I haven't gotten to see the final results yet, but what I've seen in the last twelve years makes me answer with a resounding yes. God has used my life for his glory in ways I could never have imagined before Jill was born. Because of her, McLean Bible Church has become one of the leading churches in America in the realm of ministry to people with disabilities, especially children. We minister to hundreds of these children and their families on a monthly basis, providing every imaginable service to support and encourage them.

We're now in the process of developing a Christ-centered, overnight respite center for children with disabilities and their families. It's the first of its kind in the United States, and we hope to see it become the model for a nationwide network of similar centers. None of this would have happened had it not been for God blessing us with Jill. She has opened my eyes to the special needs that these children and their families face every day.

It would be easy to say, "Lon, this is wonderful, but is it fair that Jill has to live a life of suffering so that you can be a greater servant and the work of God can move forward?"

Believe me, I have asked that question more times than can be numbered. And here are my answers. Jill doesn't know she's disabled. She's content, happy, and knows that Brenda and I love her deeply. She understands that her brothers, her caregivers, and hundreds of people who know her at our church love her too. Jill's every need is met and she wants for nothing. Were Jill able to speak, she would tell us that she doesn't feel the unfairness about her life that we judge to be there.

More importantly, I believe what the Bible tells us, that God doesn't settle all accounts here on earth. Some are settled on the other side, in heaven. I believe Jill's illness is not an accident or a random act of fate but God's perfect plan for her life and mine. And I believe God has a great reward awaiting Jill in heaven because she was willing to live the life he chose for her so his purposes could be realized on earth. In heaven, not only will Jill be healed and whole for all eternity, but she will enjoy heavenly rewards that I can only imagine. God is going to exalt Jill, and those of us who served her on earth are going to be really glad we did when we get to heaven.

You might say, "Lon, you are such a simple man. How can anyone have something as complex as Jill's sickness, and its accompanying tragedy, tied up so neatly?"

Well, I believe that God's answers for life, as expressed in the Bible, are often quite simple. It's all based on believing God's promises and then trusting him with all our heart.

As Proverbs 3:5-6 says, "Trust in the Lord, with all your heart, and lean not on your own understanding; in all your ways acknowledge him, and he *will* make your paths straight."

It's a simple but powerful strategy that has served God's servants well for millennia. You can make it more complicated if you wish, but I'll stick with the way the Lord said to do it.

DISCUSSION QUESTIONS

1. What kind of an approach to life does it take for a person to embrace the idea that a valuable

product is worth a difficult process? To what degree do you posses this approach to life? How do you think you could improve in this area?

2. How intimate would you say that your relationship with God is?

3. Evaluate yourself, with one being the lowest and ten the highest, when it comes to the following characteristics:
   - Approachability
   - Teachability
   - Sensitivity to people
   - Turflessness
   - Forgiving spirit

4. Before you read this book, what were your thoughts about why God's Spirit is not moving in our world today like he has in the past? How has this book changed your thoughts on this issue?

*The church has always been at its strongest
when blessed with strong leaders
who knew the power and anointing
of Almighty God upon their lives.*

~J. Oswald Sanders, *Spiritual Leadership*~

EPILOGUE

ON TO
HIGHER GROUND

In my twenty-five years as a pastor, I've been called upon to perform scores of funeral services for people of every age, race, and socio-economic condition. I normally urge the family to pick hymns that they or their deceased relative found meaningful. Without a doubt, the hymn most frequently chosen has been "It Is Well with My Soul."

The history of the hymn's origin is a fitting conclusion to our study on brokenness, for without a crushing experience, it would never have been written. Its author, Horatio Gates Spafford, was a prominent Chicago lawyer and real estate developer. He had a devoted wife, Anna, and four daughters, ages nine months to nine years old. Horatio and Anna were students of the Bible and had a deep personal faith in Jesus Christ.

They were also well known throughout the city for their philanthropic work.

Mr. Spafford was a good friend and ardent supporter of Dwight L. Moody, the greatest evangelist of that day. Horatio and Anna were faithful members of the Fullerton Avenue Presbyterian Church, which they helped build. Horatio was an elder there and also took part in a variety of other Christian endeavors. He served twice as the director of the Presbyterian Theological Seminary of the Northwest and, with Moody, started the famous "Noon Prayer Meeting," where business and professional men from across Chicago met each weekday to pray. Spafford helped set Moody on his career by getting him out of debt in 1870 so Moody could preach full time. During the great Chicago fire of 1871, the Spaffords worked for months as members of the Relief Aid Committee and let refugees from the blaze stay in their home.

In 1873, the Spaffords decided to take a vacation to Europe. They booked passage on the SS *Ville du Havre*, the most luxurious ocean liner of the day. But just before departure, Horatio received an offer from a man who wanted to buy land in Chicago. He sent his wife and four daughters ahead and planned to join them in France.

Several days into the voyage across the Atlantic, their ship was rammed in the middle of the night by a merchant vessel. It sank in twelve minutes. Anna and her four daughters clutched each other on the deck as the ship went down. The violence of the rushing water tore all four children from Anna's grasp. She was found floating unconscious on a piece of debris almost an hour later and rescued. The bodies of her four daughters were never found. When she reached Wales, she cabled her husband in Chicago these two words, "Saved alone."

Horatio Spafford was inconsolable. He had lost everything in the Chicago fire and now the sea had taken his four daughters. He was wracked with confusion over the deaths of his children. What had he and Anna done to deserve such a tragedy? Sailing across the Atlantic to meet his wife, Horatio asked the captain to notify him when they reached the spot where his daughters drowned. Around 2 a.m. on a December morning in 1873, the ship sailed over the watery graves of his children. As he stood on the deck, Spafford reached in his coat pocket and discovered an envelope. Standing under dim light, he began to write down his thoughts:

> When peace, like a river, attendeth my way,
> When sorrows like sea billows roll,
> Whatever my lot, Thou hast taught me to say
> It is well, it is well, with my soul.
> Though Satan should buffet, though trials should
>   come,
> Let his blest assurance control,
> That Christ hath regarded my helpless estate,

And hath shed his own blood for my soul.
My sin, oh, the bliss of this glorious thought!
My sin – not in part but the whole,
Is nailed to the cross, and I bear it no more,
Praise the Lord, praise the Lord, O my soul!
And Lord, haste the day when my faith shall be
  sight,
The clouds be rolled back as a scroll,
The trump shall resound, and the Lord shall
  descend—
Even so, it is well with my soul.

Philip Bliss, the famous songwriter, soon put Stafford's words to music, and "It Is Well with My Soul" became an immediate favorite among Christ-followers across the world.

God used a shattering brokenness experience to produce a hymn that has comforted and given solace to untold millions of souls since 1873. Let me reiterate. This hymn was not produced through success but through painful loss and suffering. It was birthed in the womb of brokenness. That's the message of this book — that God's greatest works have come from broken people like Horatio Gates Spafford.

This experience changed the Spaffords forever. Anna knew she was spared from drowning with her daughters for a reason. As a result, she dedicated her life to the service of Christ. Shortly after the accident, Horatio went on to write these words:

> Long time I dared not say to thee,
> O Lord, work thou thy will with me.
> But now so plain thy love I see,
> I shrink no more from sorrow.

A FINAL CHALLENGE

I end with a challenge: step out of the murky shadowlands of churchianity to pursue true usefulness and power with God. I challenge you to reject the play-it-safe brand of Christianity that is so popular today and to embrace the kind of total surrender to God that every powerful servant of Christ has embraced. I challenge you to volunteer for whatever brokenness the Lord feels you need in order for your life to become truly useful and significant in God's hands.

Remember, no one who has been broken by God ever regretted it. Moody said, "I would not now be placed back where I was before that blessed experience if you would give me all the world."

The Apostle Paul said, "Therefore I will boast all the more gladly about my weaknesses, so that Christ's power may rest on me" (2 Cor. 12:9b).

If you're in the midst of being broken and it looks awfully bleak on the human level — or if you're afraid to volunteer for brokenness because it looks awfully tough on the human level — then God has a message of encouragement for you: keep your eyes firmly fixed on the reward ahead. Remember, the product *is* worth the process. Brokenness *is* the path to higher ground.

You may not see how God is going to bring all this to pass but you can rest in the singular truth that "...God, who does not lie, promised..." (Titus 1:2). God has never lied to anyone and he's not about to begin with you. God will make good on his promises about brokenness to you.

If we will walk with God with unquestioning trust, God will bring us through triumphantly. He has never and can never fail those who trust him without hesitation.

> I will exalt you, O LORD, for you have lifted me out of the depths and did not let my enemies gloat over me...weeping may remain for a night, but rejoicing comes in the morning...You have turned my wailing into dancing; you removed my sackcloth and clothed me with joy, that my heart may sing to you and not be silent.
> (*Ps. 30, excerpted*)

God will give this same testimonial to every Christ-follower who allows him to break and remake them. May God give you the grace to believe him and to yearn for higher ground. May God give you courage, like

Abraham's, to launch into unknown territory with only God's call to brokenness and his promises to support you. The territory may be unknown to you but not to him who calls you. As the old hymn says, "my Lord knows the way through the wilderness. All I have to do is follow."

I'm pressing on the upward way,
New heights I'm gaining every day;
Still praying as I'm onward bound,
"Lord, plant my feet on higher ground."

My heart has no desire to stay,
Where doubts arise and fears dismay;
Though some may dwell where these abound,
My prayer, my aim, is higher ground.

I want to scale the utmost heights,
And catch a gleam of glory bright;
But still I'll pray till heaven I've found,
"Lord, lead me on to higher ground."

Lord, lift me up and let me stand,
By faith on heaven's table land,
A higher plane than I have found;
Lord, plant my feet on higher ground.

Johnson Oatman, Jr., *Higher Ground*

ACKNOWLEDGMENTS

I want to thank the people who made this book a reality. At the top of the list is my special little girl, Jill. It was because of her that I learned the important lessons this book is based on. For that, I can't thank her enough.

My wife Brenda was a constant source of encouragement and support. I am forever thankful to her. I also wish to thank my three sons, James, Justin, and Jon, for their understanding, patience, and solidarity over the last thirteen years as we've weathered the storm together. And I am grateful to my friend and publisher, Greg Vistica, whose stamina and hard work was largely responsible for getting this book to press. His editorial help was invaluable in preparing the manuscript for publication.

Thanks to Bob Eckhart, the faithful street preacher

in Chapel Hill, North Carolina, whom the Lord sent just for me in 1971.

I want to also thank those men who believed in me as a young Christ follower, and who gave me a chance to serve the Lord when so many others wouldn't: Rev. Bob Porter, Dr. William Simmer, Dr. Homer Heater, Dr. R. Herbert Fitzpatrick, and Rev. Marlin "Butch" Hardman.

I want to express my appreciation to two authors who have preceded me in dealing with this subject and whose ideas were invaluable. The first is Watchman Nee and his book, *The Release of the Spirit*. Dr. Charles Stanley picked up where Nee left off in his tape series called "Brokenness" and his book, *The Blessings of Brokenness*. I am grateful for the inspiration that these authors provided me.

Thanks to my close friend Tim LaHaye, who urged me onward at every point and was kind enough to write this book's foreword.

Thanks to Joni Eareckson Tada, Dave Dravecky, Dr. Jerry Falwell, and David Brickner for their kind words of endorsement and their comradeship in the service of Jesus Christ.

Lastly, I so appreciate my good friend, Dan McKinnon, who has been urging and prodding me for over ten years to "do a book." Well, Dan, here it is!

ABOUT
THE AUTHOR

Lon Solomon was born and raised in a Jewish home in Portsmouth, Virginia. While majoring in chemistry at the University of North Carolina, Chapel Hill, Lon's life became a relentless search for meaning and purpose. He tried to fill the void with fraternity life, partying, and gambling. Eventually he developed a serious drinking problem. When all this failed to supply the inner peace he was seeking, Lon became deeply involved in drugs, both as a user and a distributor.

Lon then turned to "spiritual" things — including psychedelics. He tried Eastern religions and a return to mainstream Judaism. When all this failed, Lon decided that suicide was the only reasonable way out. It was then that Lon met a street evangelist in Chapel Hill who began to talk to him about Jesus Christ. After months of interaction with this man, Lon made the decision to accept Jesus as his personal Savior and Messiah in the spring of 1971.

Lon is a marvelous example of God's transforming power in action. After Lon's decision to accept Christ, he was able to quit the drug and alcohol abuse that had plagued his life for years. Lon went on to graduate from Capital Bible Seminary in Old Testament with highest honors. He then did his graduate work at Johns Hopkins University in Near Eastern Studies. He taught Hebrew and Old Testament at Capital Seminary from 1975–1980.

In 1980 Lon became the senior pastor at McLean Bible Church in the Virginia suburbs of Washington, D. C. Today, Lon ministers to over 10,000 people every weekend at McLean Bible Church. McLean's innovative ministry includes:

- Frontline, a ministry targeted to Generation X, that has grown to 2,000 weekly participants seven years from its inception;
- The House, a ministry to teenagers in southeast Washington, D.C., that provides after-school, weekend, and summer programs focused around spiritual growth, character formation, and skill training;
- Access, the largest church ministry to children with special needs and their families in the Washington, D.C., area; and

- The Gathering, a generational-based ministry for those in their late teens and early twenties, that has grown to 500 young people weekly.

Lon has been on the board of Jews for Jesus since 1987; he now serves as chairman of the board's executive committee. In September 2002 Lon was appointed by President George W. Bush to serve in his administration as a member of the President's Committee on Mental Retardation.

Lon and his wife, Brenda, have been married for twenty-eight years. They have four children, Jamie, Justin, Jonathan, and Jill. They live in Fairfax, Virginia.

Lon's thirty-minute Sunday radio broadcast called "So What?" can be heard weekly on WAVA-FM (105.1), WJFK-FM (106.7), WASH-FM (97.1), WWZZ-FM (104.1), WBIG-FM (100.3) and WMZQ-FM (98.7) in the Washington, D.C. area as well as WGMD-FM (92.5) on Maryland's Eastern Shore. Lon also has sixty-second radio spots called "Not a Sermon, Just a Thought" that air on ten secular radio stations in the D.C. area. These spots prompt non-Christian listeners, in language that makes sense to them, to think about the validity of the Christian message for their lives.

"So What?" characterizes the essence of Lon's message. What difference does the Bible make for our lives in the twenty-first century? He often says that a pastor is no good unless he answers the questions "so what?" and "how?" for people. His practical, humorous, and down-to-earth treatment of scripture is refreshing, entertaining, and challenging. After you hear Lon speak, you'll always be able to answer the question, "So what?"

RED DOOR
PRESS